Stories from Below the Poverty Line

Stories from Below the Poverty Line

Urban Lessons for Today's Mission

George D. Beukema

Foreword by Jim Wallis

Herald
Press

Scottdale, Pennsylvania
Waterloo, Ontario

Library of Congress Cataloguing-in-Publication Data
Beukema, George D., 1955-
    Stories from below the poverty line : urban lessons for today's mission /
George D. Beukema.
        p. cm.
    ISBN 0-8361-9143-9 (alk. paper)
        1. Church work with the poor—United States. 2. Church work with
    minorities—United States. 3. Beukema, George D., 1955- I. Title

    BV639.P6 B48 2001
    261.8'325—dc21   00-053992

The paper used in this publication is recycled and meets the minimum require-
ments of American National Standard for Information Sciences—Permanence
of Paper for Printed Library Materials, ANSI Z39.48-1984.

STORIES FROM BELOW THE POVERTY LINE
Copyright © 2001 by Herald Press, Scottdale, Pa. 15683
        Published simultaneously in Canada by Herald Press,
        Waterloo, Ont. N2L 6H7. All rights reserved
Library of Congress Catalog Number: 00-053992
International Standard Book Number: 0-8361-9143-9
Printed in the United States of America
Book design by Merrill R. Miller, Herald Press, in collaboration with Michael
    A. King, Pandora Press U.S.
Cover design by Merrill R. Miller. Cover photo by Wallowitch

11 10 09 08 07 06 05 04 03 02   10 9 8 7 6 5 4 3 2

To order or request information, please call
1-800-759-4447 (individuals); 1-800-245-7894 (trade).
Website: www.mph.org

To
my mother and father,
who taught me how to lose my self
so I might find it

Contents

Foreword

Amid the most amazing prosperity the world has ever seen, one in six out of all children in the United States remains in poverty and one in three among children of color. On the frontlines of those struggling to overcome this persistent poverty amid plenty are faithful Christians serving the poor in urban communities. They minister to the immediate needs of people and raise their voices for economic justice.

In this book George Beukema both ministers and calls for justice. From East Harlem to Cleveland to Chicago, his gift of listening to and telling stories opens the door for deeper spiritual and political truths. It is a chronicle of one man's journey to understanding, but it contains broader lessons for us all.

That personal chronicle illustrates another truth. To change our communities, we must first change our thinking. For that to happen, we must experience firsthand the world we wish to change.

Real change begins to happen when we cross the normal boundaries of our lives to experience a different reality. That's the first step. When you leave your comfortable space and step out into a new one, you make new discoveries. You learn things you never would in a university or seminary.

The people I know who are committed to working on issues of poverty say that their transformation took place when they first went to a two-thirds world country or to an inner city neighborhood in North America. In those worlds very different from their own, they had "conversion experiences" that shaped the rest of their lives.

Beukema had the beginnings of that conversion at age nine when his father moved the family from Holland, Michigan, to a parish in East Harlem. One year later, they moved to the inner city of Cleveland, where his education continued. These experiences led Beukema to an urban, multicultural congregation in Chicago, the city within which he continues to minister.

Throughout that journey, Beukema learned about approaching a community as a servant rather than one who knows all the answers, about the richness of community life, and about the vitality of faith among the urban poor. These lessons led to his reflections on sin, anger, grace, and salvation. In the stories of Chicago's homeless and the observations of college and seminary students who participated in urban service programs, Beukema's righteous indignation and commitment to change shine forth.

George Beukema concludes that "For the church to bring the gospel to our increasingly urban world, we need the eyes to see, the ears to hear, and the courage to cross our Jordan. Our salvation lies on the other side."

On the other side remains the guiding vision of God's kingdom—a kingdom where the poor and the affluent are blessed through new relationships with each other and with God. In Isaiah's words, when we offer our food to the hungry and satisfy the needs of the afflicted, our light shall rise in the darkness, and *our* healing comes quickly.

—Jim Wallis, editor of Sojourners *and convener of*
Call to Renewal, a national federation of churches and
faith-based organizations working to overcome poverty.

Preface

At an urban conference about ten years ago a gentleman said to me, "It's always good to meet another bicultural minister." As the word *bicultural* was spoken, a clearer understanding of my life's story and vocation began to emerge.

I am Anglo, male, college- and seminary-educated, employed, and a homeowner. I live far above the poverty line. Yet I spent most of my childhood and youth living among the poor on Cleveland's Near West Side. I have spent eight years as a pastor in a low-income housing development on Chicago's North Side and ten years as an instructor bringing college students into inner-city Chicago neighborhoods to listen and learn about matters of urban life and faith.

I live and work between the worlds of affluence and poverty. In this sense, I am bicultural. It is from this peculiar vantage point, and the particular places mentioned above, that the following stories and reflections come.

In general, this book is written for Christians who care—specifically about matters of poverty, justice, and peace. In particular, this book is written for those who desire to serve, or are preparing to serve, in culturally and economically diverse communities.

Perhaps more than anything else, I hope that the book will inspire a deep appreciation and respect for the vitality of faith in urban poor communities. Yet I hope that these stories will also inspire action for reforming the systems and structures of our society that are taking the life out of communities, whether rich or poor. Such changes are not only in the interest of the poor who stand in physical need of daily bread, but also for persons and communities who are starving spiritually amid their overabundance.

The living Bread that is Jesus Christ, for whom we all hunger, is incarnational—both social and personal, material and spiritual. All persons and communities need this Bread in its fullness. Many who live below the poverty line understand this. This book aims to help those living above the poverty line to reach the same understanding.

I have come to see with increasing clarity how critical it will be for the church to bridge the divide between rich and poor, urban and non-urban, if it hopes to provide a vital witness in the twenty-first century. Such a coming together is not only in the interest of the poor, who need the resources of the affluent, but also of the affluent, who need the resources of the poor. Quite simply, we need each other. It is my deep hope that this book will inspire local, church-based initiatives for establishing partnerships between urban and non-urban Christians and their respective ministries.

As all communities of our society, including small towns, small cities, suburbs, and rural areas, become increasingly urbanized and multicultural, we would do well to learn new ways of being the church that are more relevant to, and respectful of, persons of diverse economic levels and cultural backgrounds. Tomorrow, if not today, such persons will quite literally be our neighbors.

We must break down the false divisions that fool us into believing rich and poor are more different than alike. The hope for the church resides in a gospel that proclaims unity amid diversity. It is my prayer that this book will invigorate hope for this kind of unity.

Theologian Abraham Heschel states, "Human solidarity is not the product of being human; being human is the product of human solidarity. . . . The degree to which one is sensitive to other people's suffering, to another's humanity, is the index of one's own humanity." And in the words of the apostle Paul, "There is no longer Jew nor Greek, there is no longer slave nor free, there is no longer male nor female; for all of you are one in Christ Jesus." At this time in history, this may be the greatest lesson of all that is ours to learn.

This book has been in the brooding stage for a long time. Renderings of the stories that follow have found their way into my sermons, articles, lectures, and conversations over the last sixteen years. Only recently have parishioners, students, colleagues, and friends encouraged me to bring these stories together in this form.

I am indebted to these good friends as well as the many urban residents whose lives and witness provide this book's substance; to members of the Calvary Reformed Church in Cleveland, for it was with these friends and neighbors that I learned as a young boy to find God in the most unexpected places; and to the members of the Church of the Good News and the Lathrop Homes public housing development in Chicago.

In particular I thank Maynard Batie and his family, Sharon Schramel, Letitia Lehmann, Lesszest George, Ray Ponce, Zsame Lawrence, Mae McKnight, Rev. Liala Ritsema Beukema, and many others. From them I received the kind of education that shaped, challenged, and sharpened my understanding of ministry by revealing the power that comes when we unite our love for God with our love for community.

I am also indebted to the students of nine Midwestern colleges: Hope (Holland, Michigan); Calvin (Grand Rapids, Michigan); Northwestern (Orange City, Iowa); Dordt (Sioux City, Iowa); Central (Pella, Iowa); Trinity (Palos Heights, Illinois); Briar Cliff (Sioux Center, Iowa); Aquinas (Grand Rapids, Michigan) and Spring Arbor (Spring Arbor, Michigan). Over the last ten years I have been privileged to teach students from these schools through the Chicago Metropolitan Center, a Christian-college work-study program. I have learned that the longing of these students for meaning and liberation, though different from that of the poor, is every bit as deep and real.

I give thanks to the scholars and educators whose ideas helped to clarify the significance and meaning of my experiences. In particular I am indebted to the work of sociologist John McKnight (Chapter 2), economists Jeremy Rifkin and Juliet Schor, and theologian Walter Wink (Chapter 7). Foundational to this book are the works of Walter Brueggemann (in particular *The Creative Word: The Canon as Model for Biblical Education*), anthropologist Paul Hiebert, missiologists Lesslie Newbigin and George Hunsberger, educators Paulo Freire and Parker Palmer, and poet, painter, essayist, novelist, and farmer Wendell Berry.

I must thank those who helped me put the stories to paper. I thank Tom Boogaart and George Hunsberger, professors at Western Theological Seminary, Holland, Michigan, who scrutinized my Doctor of Ministry dissertation and accepted only my best work. Many of the stories first found their way to paper through this project.

I am indebted to James I. Cook, retired professor of Western Theological Seminary, who not only encouraged me to write this book but also provided editorial assistance, without which I am certain the manuscript would never have found favor with a publishing house. And I am indebted to the editorial staff of Herald Press, who not only saw the value in this book but increased its usefulness through their hard work.

Most of all, I am indebted to my wife Liala, my daughter Tessa, and my son Jesse, whose unceasing support provided me the constant assurance that my stories were worth telling.

Stories from Below the Poverty Line

CHAPTER 1

Courage

*I hereby command you: Be strong and
courageous; do not be frightened or dismayed, for
the Lord your God is with you wherever you go.*
—Joshua 1:9

East Harlem, New York, 1965

We piled out of our Chevy station wagon onto the hot
asphalt. Leaving us curbside, my parents checked on the
parsonage.

In the blink of an eye, children closed in around us,
blocking our view of all but the tops of the tenement
houses. Our little white hands reached toward the twists
and turns of their dark curls, while strands of blonde slid
down their thin black fingers.

"There's sticky stuff in your hair," my little sister said.

"Y'all got gold in your hair," replied the little girl.

Soon four children from Holland, Michigan, were
learning to "double-dutch" on the streets of East Harlem.

It was my father's decision to leave Michigan for the
summer. The father of my friend Tommy managed a warehouse. Jimmy's father was a teacher. The father of my
best friend, Peter, was the president of Hope College.

But my father didn't have a job. He had a calling. His was a call to the inner city. Rather than spend our last Holland summer on the beaches of Lake Michigan or in the fields playing softball with the migrant farmers who worked the nearby blueberry farms, we were off to New York, where my father would receive urban ministry training in the nation's biggest city.

On our first Sunday in East Harlem, clad in a short-sleeved white button-down shirt and bow tie, I climbed the church stairs with my mother, three sisters, and baby brother to hear my father preach. It didn't take long to figure out that this was a different kind of church.

In my Michigan church, parishioners beelined for their pews at five minutes to the hour, as though their salvation depended entirely on a timely start. Here, the clock didn't seem to matter. Scooting over to make room for latecomers, I asked my mother if next Sunday we could come after the sermon. I thought it was a good idea. She didn't.

Resplendent in robes of full color, the choir energetically sang. Through the entire service they sang, making the sermon, and even the congregational prayer, worth my attention.

At first I didn't think people liked my father's preaching. They kept interrupting him with phrases like, "Say it again," and "Tell it over," and "Preach it louder." Talking during the sermon was considered rude in my Michigan church—you wouldn't dare interrupt the pastor or he would give you the evil eye. Here, my mother explained, it was just people's way of listening.

I welcomed the Harlem summer mornings on the parsonage stairs. Watching all the people go about their business, I thought of my grandmother's parting words as she huddled my sisters and me around her lap: "You are going on a very special mission—to a very special place. You are going to save the coloreds."

At the time, I dared not ask what she meant by "the coloreds." But looking out from my perch on the parsonage steps, I figured she was referring to the people with dark skin that surrounded me. My parents called them "Blacks" or "Afro-Americans." My parents explained that this was what the people preferred to be called.

What my grandmother meant by "saving" them, I wasn't quite certain either. The best I could figure, she was speaking about their need for Jesus—something she talked about all the time. I couldn't help but smile just thinking how pleased my grandmother would be to know that the people in East Harlem already knew about Jesus and that they seemed a lot more excited about him than anyone in my church back home.

Every morning I looked for Jimmy. Sometimes he'd sneak up on me and shout, "Hey, where's my best buddy?"

"Right here!" I'd shout back, and my nine-year-old legs would spring from the ground for a quick round with the "champ."

Jimmy was a Golden Gloves boxer. On Sundays he would carry me into Sunday school on his shoulders before telling us about God's love for the world. "Red and yellow, black and white, they are precious in his sight" is what he always said.

Like his mother—always "Mrs. Mitchell" to us— Jimmy was very involved in the church. He taught Sunday school, served as a deacon, and sang in the choir. Every Saturday evening he would help his mother prepare the bulletins for Sunday morning.

The church was more their home than their home. My father would say, "The Mitchells *are* the church in East Harlem."

I didn't sleep well in the parsonage. The nights in East Harlem were even louder than the days, and having to share a room with my sisters didn't help matters.

But one evening I was glad to have them close to me. It was the evening we heard crying come from the kitchen. Straining to hear what the commotion was about, I heard someone say "stabbing." Someone else said "murder." But it wasn't until I heard Mrs. Mitchell cry out, "My baby, my baby is gone! Oh Reverend, my baby is gone," that I understood something terrible had happened. In the morning my mother told me that Jimmy was dead.

It was during the funeral when I learned that a boy named Manny had murdered Jimmy in a schoolyard. Manny was fifteen. His family had only recently moved from Puerto Rico to East Harlem.

A few days after Jimmy's funeral, I walked with my father to the corner for a newspaper. We crossed the street, our few steps spanning nations as we moved from Black Harlem to Spanish Harlem.

"Hello, Father" and "Ev'nin' Father" came the greetings from the boys who paused from drumming their congas as we passed before them.

"Hello boys," my father responded.

I asked him why they called him that. He told me it was because of his collar, and that that was what they called a minister in East Harlem. I held his hand more tightly, perhaps a small protest for having to share him with the neighborhood in this way.

I asked why Manny had killed Jimmy. My father told me that Jimmy was trying to stop the fighting that was going on between his friends and Manny's friends. My father said he really didn't know why it happened—it was hard to explain. Then he picked me up and placed me on his shoulders. I remember wanting never to come down.

Later that evening I stared at the water stains on the bedroom ceiling and thought of Jimmy. "Red and yellow, black and white, they are precious in his sight"—his words ran through my head.

Jimmy loved everybody. He was trying to help stop the fighting. Jimmy was the church in East Harlem. It didn't make sense.

I looked at the picture that hung over the dresser near the foot of my bed. It was quite different from the one hanging in my Sunday school room in Michigan. This Jesus was dark, and his face was full of lines and scruffy marks. His head tilted up and his mouth hung open like he was either laughing or crying, I couldn't tell which. I figured that this must be the Jesus of East Harlem— Jimmy's Jesus.

I prayed to this Jesus, asking him to take care of Jimmy. I rolled to my side and closer to my little sister, pushed my face into my pillow and thought about home, my best friend Peter, and the Hope College pine grove.

Holland, Michigan, 1964

Peter and I stood motionless, squeezed between the tall wooden fence and the bushes that marked the boundary between his backyard and the Hope College pine grove. Our position rendered us invisible from any direction.

Only in certain places were the bushes surrounding Peter's fence thick enough to hide two boys. But we knew all the right places. We knew exactly where to view the campus "makeout" spots and the best times of day to find our prey. We knew every escape route, every turn that allowed us to disappear through the trees and shrubs at a moment's notice. This was our domain. Wearing our fatigues, face paint, and James Bond decoder rings, and carrying our cap guns from Woolworth's, there was nothing we couldn't do. We owned the pine grove.

Peter spotted the couple first. I changed my position in hopes of a better view. We watched until my gasp gave us away.

Dashing off, we hurriedly made our way to the "Whisper Bench," so designated by a bronze plaque riveted to its side. The bench was solid concrete and shaped like a half moon. Peter spoke softly, his words barely audible. Yet every syllable could be heard perfectly. It was the miracle that always happened on the bench. I whispered back. When we tired of the game, we raced on to the Six Flavors ice cream parlor on College Avenue and Seventh Street.

The pine grove was more than a site for our subversive activities. It was a place for picnics in the summer and concerts in the fall. The grove had a tall, steep hill for sledding during Holland's snowy, lake-effect winters.

Most important, the pine grove was where I launched the balloon that put me on the front page of the Holland *Evening Sentinel*.

I remember the day Mr. Duggan delivered the letter. At first my mother didn't think it was for me, because I never got mail, except a birthday card from my grandmother.

I rushed to my mother's side, my hands in a flutter as she scrutinized the envelope. She was still thinking it must be for my father, since we have almost the same name. But the envelope was not addressed to him but to George Duane Beukema—me.

Wanting to get in on the action, my sisters tightened their circle around me and the envelope. I dropped to my knees to keep them away and opened it quickly, careful not to damage anything valuable inside.

I was hoping it was the magnifying glass I had sent away for months earlier. Every day for weeks I had tried to wish my package into Mr. Duggan's blue bag.

Instead, I found a letter. Unfolding it, I looked at the scratchy writing. Being only in the fourth grade, I asked my mother for help:

Dear Dr. Beukema,
I hope this reaches you in time as I think your project may be important. I was plowing my field when I saw something red flapping in the breeze on my fence. I found the enclosed items. I guessed you wanted them back. Good luck in your research.
—*John Bussman*

He had found my balloon. Better yet, he called me "doctor." At that moment I was convinced I was a doctor, deserved to be a doctor, and was destined to be one.

I ran out the door to show the letter to Mrs. Vander Werf, who was Peter's mother and my Cub Scout den mother. It had been three months since Cub Scout Pack No. 5 launched its thick red balloons in the pine grove.

It was Mrs. Vander Werf's best idea ever, a contest to see whose balloon would be returned from the farthest distance. We filled the balloons with helium from the tanks in the college science lab, each tagged with a message that read, "Please return promptly to addressee."

Before launching the balloons, we spoke the Cub Scout pledge with the kind of reverence we gave the Apostles' Creed. It was torture not being allowed to let the balloons fly the moment we hit the outdoors. But I followed directions.

As painful as it often was, I always followed directions. My father would explain that there is a right way and a wrong way to do everything and that there is a place for everything and everything should remain in its place.

Yet it's hard to leave the familiar. That night in East Harlem, I thought of my father's words, that there's a place for everything and everything should remain in its place. I believed he was right and wanted nothing more than to remain in Holland; a place of innocent play in a pine grove; a place where a newspaper reports even a simple story like the excitement of a boy and his returned balloon; a place of comfort and familiarity. I prayed that God would either change my father's call or let him get a normal job.

Cleveland, 1967

"Winston Tastes Good Like A Cigarette Should" claimed the billboard posted to the side of the Desk Exchange building on the corner of Sixty-Fifth and Fur Avenue, just across the street and a few houses down from the parsonage. The junior high hangout behind the building was simply called "The Exchange." It was the gathering place of the many who became my friends my first year in Cleveland. They weren't considered a gang like the boys on Fifty-Seventh Street who had the schoolyard as their hangout. My group of friends were simply known in the neighborhood as "Sixty-Fifth" and The Exchange was their hallowed ground. It was there that I met Mickey.

Mickey was tall, dark, and handsome—at least the girls thought so, and if boys were allowed to admit something like this, all would have agreed. His straight black hair hung just below his shoulders and with a quick shake of the head he would bring it to perfect order, a ritual he enacted every minute or two. Mickey was cool. He could also be pretty mean, so you wanted to be on his good side. I felt lucky the day Mickey invited me to his party.

I left the parsonage in creased pants, button-down shirt, and penny loafers with dimes instead of pennies—a fashion tip received from my big sister. I preferred more casual dress, but my mother demanded I wear what she was sure would be appropriate attire for an occasion like a sixth-grade graduation party.

Unlike the parsonage, Mickey's house matched the neighborhood. Its deteriorating side porch made it look as though it were proposing to the boarded-up house next door—the two making a perfect couple, though certainly not a match made in heaven. But they fit in with the neighborhood far more than a boy dressed in creased pants, a button-down shirt, and penny loafers with dimes instead of pennies.

"Come on in, kid. Party's in there, beer's in here. Make yourself at home," said Mickey's father as he pushed a bottle my way.

I clutched the beer bottle, as though my grip could keep my knees from buckling. Peter's had been my most recent party. Beyond the usual birthday cake, there were balloons, games, and prizes. Tammy, Peter's collie, came wearing a party hat made specially for her narrow head.

I knew there would be no making myself at home at this party. Beer firmly in hand, I walked through the kitchen and into the living room. I could barely see through the smoke.

"Who's got the papers, man? Somebody gimmie the papers," said a girl wearing bell-bottom jeans and a top with more buttons undone than fastened.

She asked me if I wanted a "hit." Having no idea what she was talking about, I guessed that it was in my interest to politely turn down the offer.

"No thank you," I said, and pretended to take a swig of my beer as though I did it every day.

I searched for Mickey or anyone else I could recognize. Peering into one of the bedrooms, I found Mickey's brother. He was with a girl in a way that made me miss the innocent days of spying on college coeds.

I did an about-face and found a door that led to the basement. In the basement I found a door that led to the back yard. I followed the sidewalk to the gate that opened to the alley. I ran home, rushed through the front door, and ascended the stairs feeling like Jesus must have felt during his climb to heaven from hell. I reached the toilet bowl in time.

Chicago, 1990

It was a few days after the shooting of a nine-year-old boy in Chicago's Cabrini Green public housing development that my students and I were scheduled to visit with a group of Cabrini residents. Concerned about their safety, students organized a meeting at which they scolded me for maintaining my commitment to the visit. They said they simply would not go to Cabrini. Having only second-hand knowledge of such places from TV and other media sources, all they could imagine was a location of violence and death. The news of the young boy had confirmed their worst fears.

I entered the meeting room prepared for an attack. Student after student rose to speak, at times shout.

"How can you expect us to put ourselves in such danger?"

"My mother told me on the phone last night that if you make us go into Cabrini she will call the president of my college!"

"It said on the news last night that the gang situation in Cabrini is at its worst—that no one is safe in that community and that the buildings should be torn down!"

The complaints continued. With every ounce of discipline I could muster, I fought the desire to challenge their fear with the facts:

1. During the days and weeks following such a violent incident, the police, news media, and neighborhood watch groups would provide extra attention to the community. There would be no safer time to visit.

2. Despite outbreaks of violence such as the one that took the life of the little boy, the Cabrini Green community is about so much more than violence.

3. Especially in the wake of the killing, our resident hosts wanted desperately to break the "violence-only" stereotypes conveyed by persons who do not know them and their community. The residents wanted to tell their story about loving families and beautiful children, Head Start programs and tutoring services, beautification projects and community care groups, and residents organizing to wrestle housing management responsibilities away from a uncaring government bureaucracy.

All of this was true. But I knew unless my students had a place to put their fear, they would hear none of it.

I said, "You think I'm crazy for even thinking about bringing you into Cabrini with all the violence that goes on there. Gang wars are going on, an innocent little boy was killed by crossfire, and here I am still asking you to go ahead with this visit. You want me to know that there is no way that you are going. Is that right?"

Emphatically they nodded in agreement.

Breaking a brief silence, a student rose. "Maybe I'm alone here. But I think we all really want to go. It just seems like you're asking us to do something that isn't safe. Do you really think it would be okay for us to go?"

Sensing that the students were ready to listen, I spoke of my recent conversation with the leader of the resident group. I told of her anger at the media for portraying their community in negative terms and how, now more than ever, the residents of the community wanted the opportunity to speak. I told of her conviction that it would be an honor to the little boy who died if we gave residents a chance to tell us the real story of Cabrini. Then I explained how, from my experiences in public housing communities, this would be the safest possible time to visit.

Standing in front of the designated residential building on Saturday morning, I wondered if I would soon have to apologize to the gathering resident group for my lack of students. Then I saw the students walking toward me, right through the middle of Cabrini.

"We got a little lost," one of the students said. "But someone pointed us in the right direction."

Moving into another culture is often traumatic. In a brief moment, all that we know can be shattered into little pieces. A different landscape, language, values, and worldview leave us uncomfortable, if not terrified. In response, we quickly erect barriers in an effort to stop, or at least buffer, the onslaught of foreign realities.

How difficult it is to summon the courage for breaking through the fear of the unknown. For many people, engaging a new world is an experience of losing the self. When this happens, it is hard to believe that a new self or frame of reference will be found. Anthropologists use terms such as "freezing of boundaries" to describe defense mechanisms employed for battling the perceived enemy— the unknown.

In cross-cultural experiences, the typical stages of fear, denial, anger, and avoidance, have been well documented. Some people are able to move through and beyond these stages, while others hang on to the familiar with persistence and passion.

As psychotherapists recognize, helping a client move into, and through, a particular traumatic memory demands that the therapist provide a safe and trusting atmosphere in which the client can find courage and support. In a similar way, people who desire to enter a foreign land must find a source of courage and strength.

In the first chapter of the book of Joshua, God calls a leader to succeed Moses and to bring the people into the land of Canaan. "Be strong and courageous; do not be frightened or dismayed," God tells Joshua, "for the Lord your God is with you wherever you go."

Like Joshua we must have faith and good courage as we cross our Jordan.

CHAPTER 2

Servanthood

> *Then they came to Capernaum; and when he was in the house he asked them, "What were you arguing about on the way?" But they were silent, for on the way they had argued with one another who was the greatest. He sat down, called the twelve, and said to them, "Whoever wants to be first must be last of all and servant of all."*
> —Mark 9: 33-35

Cleveland, 1966

It was a gray summer day when our family left Michigan.

"Dear Lord," my father prayed before we started out, "we ask that you watch over and protect us from all harm. Thank you for the new home you have waiting for us in Cleveland. Be with all of our friends in Holland and keep them safe. In Jesus' name we pray. Amen."

I liked the prayers with which my father began our family trips. Not only because they were shorter than his church prayers, but also because they made me feel safe.

Cramped in the back of our Chevy wagon, I looked through the rear window feeling as dreary as the weather.

My only consolation was the bag my mother had allowed me to keep by my side instead of packing in the moving van that had gone on before us.

Using an old pillowcase and a piece of rope cleverly hemmed into the bag's opening, she had created a safe place for my valuables. These included a small bag of marbles that held my precious steely and the vast array of shooters I had won fair and square from my school friends; an army man dangling from a kite string carefully tied to four corners of my mother's blue babushka, making a perfect paratrooper; Lincoln Logs that I used not to build log houses, but as catapults for use against Peter's army of toy soldiers; and my most prized possession—a silver dollar won in a footrace. The dollar reminded me of the moment when I proved I was the fastest fifth grader in Lincoln School.

But today the bag was of little comfort. We were leaving all that seemed safe and good. I thought about what my third grade teacher, Mrs. Vander Bush, had said on the day President John F. Kennedy was killed: "Things will never be the same again."

Dwarfed only by the brown-brick structure of the Calvary Reformed Church next door, the Cleveland parsonage stood tall and proud amid the debris that was to be my new neighborhood.

My parents had explained the meaning of the word *parsonage*. Instead of old Mr. Kleis who lived on the corner of Columbia Avenue and Eleventh Street in Holland, the church would be our landlord. My mother wasn't fond of the idea of a parsonage (she told of the minister who was asked to leave a church because his wife rearranged the furniture once too often). But I liked the arrangement as soon as I discovered that the church janitor would cut the grass in the summer and shovel the walks in winter.

Our second day in the parsonage I convinced my father to help me break the padlock that kept me from exploring the contents of one of the basement rooms. "Holy Moses!" exclaimed my father at the sight of a roomful of bicycles.

A neighbor explained that over the years the former pastor had taken the bikes from neighborhood children. Whenever a bike was left on church land, the pastor would confiscate it.

Listening to neighbors provided answers to other mysteries as well, including the biggest: how a church could lose all but seven of its members in the course of a few years. The collection of bicycles provided the first clue.

Our family of seven doubled Calvary's worship attendance—a good beginning in terms of my father's plans for growth. But he knew it would take more than this to bring the church back to life.

My father figured there was no better place to start than with the bicycles. Within two weeks, every bicycle had been cleaned, repaired, and given back to children in the neighborhood. I guess you could say that it was the church's first act of community repentance and my first lesson on the value of listening to one's neighbors.

The second lesson came soon after.

I dreaded the thought of leaving the parsonage, but September had come and the school year was starting. If I said a word on my first day at Waverly Elementary, I'm sure I said it quietly.

On my way home that first day, I heard the boys call to me. They were standing against a chain-link fence that encircled one of the many weed-infested lots in the neighborhood. They asked me what I was looking at.

"Nothing," I said in as friendly a manner as possible, wanting to assure them that I was speaking nothing but the truth. I was thinking about running when he threw the punch.

I escaped with only a bruise that was slight enough to make silence about the experience an option. I decided not to worry my parents.

That night I prayed that the boys were finished making their point. But the next day, the 3:30 bell came much too soon.

"Hey, punk!"

This time I kept walking. I'm not sure why, but for some reason I figured that if I maintained a steady pace—careful not to walk too fast or too slow—they might leave me alone. This time they knocked me to the ground. One of the boys raised his foot.

This time I didn't just think about running. I jumped to my feet and exercised my sneakers to the fullest. In Holland I was fast. In Cleveland I was faster.

I considered it divine intervention that my father insisted on picking me up after school the next day, as he needed my help delivering some groceries to our neighborhood's elderly. I felt relief, but knew it was only temporary. Yet God's intervention continued in my mother's insistence that I make friends with the boy who lived across the street. His name was Ben and our mothers had become friends. I wasn't thrilled by her request, but I obeyed.

Our bike ride to Lake Erie wasn't long, but we went far enough that by the end of the day my bicycle seat had made its mark. It was tooling down Kings Hill that made the greatest impression—"the best hill in Cleveland," Ben would boast, as though the hill was his and his alone. Although biking down the hill was illegal, as indicated clearly by the signs posted, Ben explained that cops had better things to do than worry about us kids.

Pushing off with my left foot and thrusting down with my right, I plummeted downhill toward the Lake Shore Highway on the other side of the guardrail. Barely stopping in time, I felt the rush of danger and thought about Peter and the Pine Grove.

Ben had what my mother called a "potty mouth." Although the likes of his words were never to be spoken in my house, I was intrigued by their force and rhythm. While I knew that using them was wrong, they somehow seemed to make sense in this place.

Like most boys in the neighborhood, Ben came from the southern Appalachian mountain region. But, he said to me on our first day together, "I'm not a stupid hillbilly like everyone else around here." His reasoning was that his parents had moved to Cleveland from West Virginia before he was born.

Rarely did Ben say much else about his family. But I came to believe he really loved them—at least his two brothers and three sisters. He cooked their meals, helped with their homework, washed their clothes, and did just about everything else it takes to run a family. I had my chores, but Ben had a job. His mother was seldom around, and if she was, she was usually "sleeping one off," as Ben would say. Whenever I asked about his father, he changed the subject.

After our bike ride, while resting on the steps of the corner deli, Ben told me I should stop taking crap from the boys on Fifty-Seventh Street. I didn't say anything, just sat there feeling stupid while picking the chocolate coating off my ice-cream bar. He explained that they would beat me up every day unless I showed them something. I said I didn't want to fight. Truth be known, I didn't know how to fight—it was something not covered in my Cub Scout manual.

He rose from the stoop. "See, ya gotta look bad, man. Ya gotta walk like this."

He strutted around our bikes with his arms swaying and head twitching. I stopped laughing when he made me practice. This time, he laughed. Then he gave me the best gift of all—an invitation to walk to and from school with him and his friends.

For the first time I thought maybe I was going to be okay. It pays to listen to your neighborhood.

Chicago, 1985

It was during a church board meeting that they stormed into the room demanding answers. Unsure as to why the group of Lathrop residents would be making such a fuss, I asked the reason for their visit.

"It's about this Lifelines program. They've been here before, you know. They come in here and tell us what's wrong with our children and our neighborhood. We heard you're working with them. Is that right?"

Because we had come to Chicago eager to serve, we were excited when the people from Lifelines, a social service organization, came to the church with their proposal. Knowing our church was well known and respected in the Lathrop Homes community, they saw us as an effective conduit for their program to help the many young girls of Lathrop who were vulnerable to pregnancy.

While it is difficult for an outsider to understand why a girl of eleven, twelve, or thirteen would choose to engage in sexual activity or refrain from taking protective measures against pregnancy, there are reasons. First, sex feels good and when there is so much that feels bad, it is no small thing to feel good, even if for only a few moments. Second, when you live in a system like public housing and rarely have control over your life, being in control of something—anything—has great appeal, especially when that something is a precious little baby. Third, along with a child may come a public assistance check.

While I have never known a mother to get rich on public assistance, a young woman achieves a certain status and feels a sense of accomplishment when she is able to get her own check and perhaps even move into her own apartment. The desire for independence is no stranger to any youth, rich or poor.

These are powerful forces. I figured that the quality of life at stake for the many young girls in Lathrop was worth a fight.

Though stunned by our community guests' interruption, I decided to throw aside Robert's Rules of Order and move this matter to the top of our church board's agenda. I explained to our guests that after talking with the social service organization in question, we planned to allow them use of our facility to launch a pregnancy prevention program for the teenage girls in our neighborhood.

Mrs. James, the community's matriarch spoke first. "So where does the money come from for this program? And where is the money they are bringing into our community going to end up—in the pockets of the people of this community or in the pockets of a bunch of do-good social workers?"

(The truth is, most social service dollars find their way into the pockets of white professionals who rarely live in the communities they serve. In fact, social service money often leaves the "client community" as fast as it comes in.)

"And what's their plan for pregnancy prevention?" another community person demanded. "Are they going to tell our children that they better just close their legs and get good grades, or are they going to help us get some new books in our school and some new teachers who really care about our kids?"

(Ninety-eight percent of the Lathrop children attend a school still using books from the 1970s. Furthermore, fear of the community prevents many teachers from getting involved in the lives of the children.)

When I saw the elders and deacons of the church board nod their heads in agreement, I knew that we had made a mistake.

We come to the Scriptures with a hermeneutic—a framework for interpreting what we read. Similarly, we come to a community with a hermeneutic—a framework for interpreting what we see.

What then is our community hermeneutic? How do we view the community we seek to serve?

In *The Careless Society*, sociologist John McKnight distinguishes between the way a good servant and a bad servant view a community. The bad servant views a community primarily in terms of its needs or deficiencies and fails to recognize that the power to label people as "needy" or declare them "deficient" is the basic tool of control and oppression.

Obscured by the mask of love and care, professional service providers sell their commodities of assistance exactly as marketers sell other products. They portray needs in ways that are marketable to the sensibilities of donors. (How easy it is to sell poverty-relief programs with pictures of bloated-belly destitution.)

Three disabling effects result from the way service professionals market needs. First, a need is depicted as a deficiency rather than a condition, a right, or an obligation of another. Second, rather than placing the problem in its full social context, the situation is depicted as a lack on the part of the client. Third, the deficiency is defined in such a way as to direct the response toward professionalized service and away from the resources of residents and their community.

Within this kind of system, clients are treated less as persons in need and more as persons needed by the system. The service provider then seeks to manufacture needs to expand the budget of the servicing system.

Well meaning Christians are vulnerable to making the same mistake. It is tempting to view poor communities through the lens of a deficiency hermeneutic. Christians then become the "full pitcher" on a mission to pour help into an "empty bucket." This perpetuates a dependency model of service in which we, the supposed experts, come into a poor community to define its needs and create programs to keep it dependent on our services. The system has a devastating effect on these communities.

By contrast, the good servant brings a hermeneutic that casts persons and communities in the light of their gifts and resources. The good servant does not use Christ's call to servanthood as a way to dominate and control. The good servant's call is not to be simply a provider of goods and services, but rather a missionary of mutuality.

A Lathrop Homes resident and member of the Church of the Good News gives this testimony:

> One of the most meaningful things about Good News is the recognition given to the gifts of the people of this community. Those of us who live in the "projects" are often overlooked in that respect. [This] church offers what social service organizations don't offer. To these organizations, people are just numbers and just people with needs. We don't assign numbers here. And people aren't seen as a bunch of "problems" walking around. This is a

place where you have a name and a purpose. You
are recognized for what you have and not for what
you lack. I'm doing things now in this church and in
our community that if someone seven or eight years
ago told me I'd being doing I'd say, "Yeah, right."
Now I'm president of the music school! I'm learning
so much about God and myself. And I'm learning
how to seek out the gifts in others.

A capacity hermeneutic affirms the God-given gifts,
knowledge, resources, and wisdom of all peoples and
communities, bearing witness to the holiness of all God's
creatures and creation. A capacity hermeneutic skirts the
temptation of locating the brokenness of a community
within the confines of personal failures and shortcomings
of the residents and makes room for a broader, more sys-
temic understanding of sin. A call to listen to one's community makes absolutely no sense at all if the community
is viewed as having nothing valuable to say.

Listening for truth and correction "from below" may
seem backwards, but we must consider how Jesus constantly got things backwards. He said that to be strong,
we must become weak and to find life, we must lose it.

In the Mark 9 passage introducing the chapter, Jesus
gets it backwards once again. Teaching his disciples a lesson on greatness, he says that to be first they must be last.
Then, in verses 36-37, he enacts a parable by bringing a
child into their circle. "Whoever welcomes one such child
in my name welcomes me," he says, "and whoever welcomes me welcomes not me but the one who sent me."

A child has no pretensions to greatness. A child is unas-
suming. This is the posture of Christian servanthood.

CHAPTER 3

Special Revelation

*He also said, "With what can we compare the
kingdom of God, or what parable will we use
for it? It is like a mustard seed, which, when sown
upon the ground, is the smallest of all the seeds on
earth; yet when it is sown it grows up and
becomes the greatest of all shrubs, and
puts forth large branches, so that
the birds of the air can make
nests in its shade."*
—Mark 4:30-32

Chicago, 1985

In Chicago's Uptown you can find just about anyone:
immigrants of all nationalities, homeless adults and children, and prostitutes, male and female, of all ages. The
halfway houses that speckle the neighborhood provide
the last support for the many disabled poor to whom the
doors to medical and psychological care facilities have
been closed.

As I walked into the mammoth building that ware-
housed hundreds, including two members of our congregation, the smell of spoiled food and human excrement

turned my stomach. With each step I scattered thousands of roaches.

I believe only by God's grace did the rickety old elevator make it to the sixth floor, where Will and Tom eagerly awaited my arrival. Greeting me in the hallway, their smiles instantly mitigated the smell of our surroundings.

They led me into their five by eight cubicle. Will insisted I take a warm cup of coffee from the hot plate that served as their stove. Tom offered me the chair that looked as if it could have belonged with three others around the kitchen table in my boyhood home in Michigan.

Before I could say a word, Will handed me a tattered Bible and asked if I would read again the Mustard Seed parable I had read in church the day before. I turned to the proper place and read the story once again.

Tom sat silently on his mattress, his eyes welling up with tears. When I finished he said, "That's me and Willy."

"What?" I said.

"The mustard seed—that's me and Willy."

As I looked at the beaten-down war veterans sitting in this small, smelly, dirty room in one of the worst neighborhoods of the city, the truth of his words hit me like a pile of bricks.

Chicago, 1986

She was a beautiful baby girl, and the service of baptism would be my first. I couldn't contain my enthusiasm, nor could her mother, her family, or the members of Good News. The meaning of baptism in the Reformed tradition—raising a child in the faith with the help of the faith family—seemed common sense to the people of Good News. Lissa, the baby's mother, would depend on her church family in ways no different from the other mothers who filled the sanctuary on Sunday mornings.

I heard someone making noise and looked out my living room window. I recognized the young man. We had had a few encounters before. Once in the Jewel food store, he flashed a stack of hundred-dollar bills in my face: "For the church, Rev. Take it, man. For my sins, you know?"

I told him we cared for him, not his money.

"But good can come out of evil. Don't you believe that, Rev?" he said, offering the money once again.

Knowing his reference was to the drug dealing that put the cash in his hands, I refused his offering once again.

My second encounter with the young man occurred one summer night when he came to the church to pick up Lissa, his girlfriend. His shirtless body showed scars from wounds I took to be from knives, bullets, or both.

Our exchange was minimal, but the impression he made was significant. Besides the fact that he terrified me, I was amazed by his knowledge of the Scriptures. He said his mother taught them to him in the days when he believed God cared for him. "Church is just a conspiracy to placate the poor masses and to empower the Man," were the words he spoke as he pulled Lissa out of the church that evening.

I opened the front door, took note of the baseball bat in his hand, and asked what he wanted. "You baptize my baby, and I will kill you and burn down the church."

I quickly closed and bolted the door, then lied to my curious children, telling them I was sure everything would be fine.

I called Lissa's family. They told me the man had just been at their home and had thrown a plank through a bedroom window. Mr. Johnson said that the young man's threat was quite clear: if we baptized his baby, he would burn the church down. Mr. Johnson asked me to come over right away.

When I arrived, the apartment was thick with family. Lissa took his threat seriously. She told of his arsenal and explained that, as the general of a major West Side gang, there was no weapon or implement of destruction he couldn't access. The guns in the hands of Lissa's brothers reaffirmed the seriousness of his threat.

Her head bowed over the baby cradled in her arms, the grandmother called us to prayer. We prayed. We prayed for refuge from the enemy. We prayed for deliverance from evil and temptation—in this case, the temptation of the older male family members to kill the man who was threatening them. We prayed for power and understanding. We prayed for safety and courage.

We prayed as if there might be no tomorrow. Breaking a period of silence the grandmother spoke from memory: "For I am sure that neither death, nor life, nor angels, nor principalities, nor things present, nor things to come, nor powers, nor height, nor depth, nor anything else in all creation, will be able to separate us from the love of God in Christ Jesus our Lord." Together we said amen.

A few hours later the police informed us that they had apprehended the young man a few blocks from the Johnson home. We thanked God for his answer.

Lissa offered a last prayer request and so before breaking the circle, we prayed for her baby's father. It was at that moment that I first realized the true identity of this young man. I had known he was the baby's father, but I had failed to acknowledge the Father that was his.

The next Sunday morning, we celebrated the baptism with lots of water. I must confess that, while dousing her little head, I looked over my shoulder more than a few times.

In seminary I took a course on administering the church sacraments and one on prayer as well. But a seminary education in a small Midwestern town is likely to come up short more than a few times when it comes to preparing one for ministry below the poverty line. To be fair, my professors had said clearly that ministry education truly begins with active ministry. They were correct.

Chicago, 1991

Earl lives in Chicago's Uptown. His home is the street and a backpack provides his shelter. The pack weighs at least fifty pounds, and its stuff sticks out at every imaginable angle: toothbrushes, toothpaste, soap and soap dish, and cloths for washing on the rare occasions that McDonalds allows him to use its restroom. Earl says local proprietors don't particularly care for people like him to bother their customers.

Stuffed into a small side pocket of the pack is a large plastic garbage bag. On rainy Chicago days, Earl pokes his head through the bottom seam. Tucked in another pocket are blades for shaving, rope for tying, thread for mending, papers and tobacco for rolling, and an umbrella with spokes that are mostly unbroken. Strapped to the side of the pack is a small grill for the times when Earl is fortunate enough to locate something meaty to barbecue.

"You've got everything in there!" a student exclaimed after Earl demonstrated the versatility of his traveling home during a discussion on homelessness.

"Almost," he replied, then went on to say that most of the items weren't his. "I carry things for my friends," Earl explained. "Maybe a third of the stuff is mine."

Not so long ago Earl worked for a Chicago railroad yard at a decent wage. And that's where it happened. Hoisting a piece of cargo onto a boxcar, he lost his balance and fell with a jolt that almost ripped the arm off his shoulder. Apparently, his years of hard work meant little to his company, and even less to those who handled his company's disability claims. The settlement he received was so small that soon after his release from the hospital, Earl was on the street.

Earl has family. But they struggle too. Earl explained their struggle as more spiritual than financial. "I can't go home," he said to a student who wondered where his family is in all of this.

That's not really true of course. More true is that he won't go home. Some of it's his pride. But it's more than that. His family has a way of beating him down, and he'd rather be in the streets than go back to that.

"Street life will knock you down and keep you down," Earl says. Disability excluded, Earl was relatively healthy until he began moving between Uptown's Argyle and Lawrence avenues. A shelter here and there helps, but he rarely sleeps. Insomnia—Earl has a bad case of it. He'll go without sleep for eight to ten days at a time. Then he "crashes." He's never sure where he'll be when he does.

"That's when my friends help out," Earl said. "You see, I carry their stuff because I'm awake most of the time. You gotta be careful on the street 'cause the minute you let down your guard, your stuff will be gone. Since I can't sleep I'm the keeper of the stuff. And then when I do crash, my friends keep a lookout. Works out pretty good—most of the time anyway."

After Earl told his story to my students, we took time for a punch and cookies break. They couldn't eat, but Earl and his friends were hungry.

Consistently, rural and suburban visitors are dumbfounded by the richness of community and the vitality of faith that they experience among Chicago's urban poor. Often, the visitors confess to a certain spiritual emptiness in their own lives and church families. While the living conditions of the urban poor may be pitied, their spiritual vitality is envied.

While I was visiting a church in a small Midwestern town, a man whose daughter had participated in a Chicago summer workcamp told me about the impact this experience had made upon his daughter and their family. His daughter called a family meeting a few days after her return from Chicago. There she retold the stories she heard from the people of the Church of the Good News and the Lathrop Homes public housing development. She shared things discussed throughout the week, during and between their work projects. In particular, she spoke of what she had learned about the biblical notion of *shalom* and its connection to the notion of justice—how well-being flows from sharing equitably in the resources of the earth. She described the incredible sense of community she discovered—how persons with so little seemed to have so much.

She told her family she wanted to experience more community and shalom in their home and church. On the kitchen table around which they were sitting she put a list of their possessions: three television sets, two stereos, two VCRs, two automobiles, two snowmobiles, skis, and on and on. She suggested each family member cross off one item for discard. She also suggested they consider spending a summer vacation doing a service project together.

At this point I wondered if the man was going to hit me or hug me for the impression this experience had made on his daughter! Instead of doing either, he simply said, "Well, we have one less television set, and we now rent our skis. And—do you do workcamps for families?"

Excerpts from letters and journals from visiting Christian brothers and sisters further illustrate the depth of spirituality among the urban poor.

I realized that the homeless, the poor, and the people living in the projects are more than just negative, hopeless statistics to be put away in a filing cabinet—they are real people with stories and powerful memories. I also realized that telling stories can be empowering not only for the listener, but the teller as well. In Uptown, Earl was delighted at the opportunity to tell his story. As he said, "I usually don't talk, but to be up here in front of you guys, and to hear you clapping is the best thing for me." But when Earl explained that only one third of the stuff in his backpack was his, and that the rest were things he carried for his homeless friends, then I realized that the homeless may know more about community than most Christians. We have much to learn from them about what it means to be the church. —*College student*

In listening to their stories I was reminded of the fundamental blessedness of people as creations of God. The undeniable power that was reflected in their stories time and time again pointed to a power bigger than them. I felt challenged because their authenticity seems to bump up against my walls, and exposes within me the fundamental ways my life inhibits connecting with others, thus, inhibiting community. —*Seminarian*

When we went into the woman's shelter, I was afraid to approach them. What if they told me to leave them alone or something worse? So I looked around and chose a little old lady to sit next to. I asked her quietly, "What are you reading?" I was nervous that maybe she'd ignore me. She said,

"Literature, biblical literature. I read literature about God because literature is crucial." (This lady was so tiny that she reminded me of my grandmother.) She then went on to explain, "I have nothing except Jesus. Jesus had nothing you know. I read his literature because I want to live like Jesus." I was so inspired by this woman. It was like she had a secret. . . . like she had a hold of something deeper than anybody else. —*Youth leader*

Before I came to Chicago I couldn't imagine what it would be like to live in the inner city. I still don't really know, but I have a better idea. I just assumed if given the chance everyone would want to live in Pella, Iowa. I was wrong. Some members of your church are better examples of truly dedicated Christians than anyone in Pella. Maybe some people have a better knowledge of the Bible, but no one demonstrates their Christianity in everything they do like some of you.

It's too easy sometimes to be a Christian in Pella when everything is going well. At your church people depend more on God to help them through everything. We, in our beautiful church, have a lot to learn. Most people, including me before this trip, have the idea that you go to the inner city to change people's lives. Instead we're leaving with our lives changed and touched in a way we'll not soon forget. —*Youth*

I sensed from the people of the Church of the Good News that they have a powerful communal experience of each other and of God. I remember one of the members saying with passion, "This is my church. And it will be my church until I die." I began to weep internally, for I desire a community that loves each other and is committed to each other in this way. In the churches I have been a part of recently, everyone knows that most members will quickly move to another church if they are not getting what they want. —*College student*

Tom's keen exegesis of the Mustard Seed parable, the Johnson family's dependency on prayer, and the community exhibited between Earl and his homeless friends, are examples of the spiritual wealth of many who live below the poverty line. They approach God with a refreshing freedom. They are "at home" with God. Theirs is a special place that makes way for a special revelation.

CHAPTER 4

Common Grace

*Then God said, "Let us make humankind in
our image, according to our likeness; and let them
have dominion over the fish of the sea, and over the
birds of the air, and over the cattle, and over all the
wild animals of the earth, and over every creeping
thing that creeps upon the earth. So God created
humankind in his image, in the image
of God he created them. . . ."*
—Genesis 1:26-27a

Cleveland, 1970

I couldn't believe it, but my sister wasn't joking. Our parents were leaving for the weekend, and she was to be in charge.

Perhaps the excitement from being asked to speak at a national mission conference had clouded my father's mind. As their car pulled away, I was off to Ricky's.

Ricky had moved about ten blocks from me and was now living in a similar neighborhood known as "Hillbilly Haven." Its boundaries were not sharply defined. But after crossing Fulton at Forty-Seventh Street, I knew I had arrived. The noise increased with the sounds of children playing on the sidewalks and in the street, mothers shouting words of discipline through open windows and doorways, and fathers banging on their broken-down cars in the streets and alleys—an activity that provided unending excuses for men to be out of their houses and out of their minds with their buddies.

Poverty is loud, but I was used to the volume by now. Only four years had passed since my move from small-town Michigan, where you could hear a pin drop on a normal day. But that time seemed like an eternity.

I entered the kitchen through the screen door and saw Ricky's legs protruding from under the kitchen sink. His brother Mickey was sitting at the kitchen table, laughing at Ricky's attempt at playing plumber. Jake stumbled into the kitchen and made stupid remarks as he took a six-pack from the refrigerator. Of the men with whom Ricky's mother kept company, Jake was not Ricky's favorite. Then again, he didn't like any of them much.

Ricky soon gave up on the sink, and we moved to the basement to practice music. I doubt there was a better time in the history of the world than 1970 to be in a band. The Rolling Stones, Grand Funk Railroad, and Creedence Clearwater Revival—we played it all and we played it loud.

Except for Ricky's drumming, the band was dreadful. Ricky's drum set, a gift from his mother's previous boyfriend, was beautiful: white pearl complete with snare, double toms, floor tom, crash, rider, and high-hat cymbals. And they were not just any cymbals, but Ziljians. Ricky's talent deserved the best.

It was well past my curfew when Ricky's mother insisted we shut down for the night. But since my parents were out of town, I decided to join Ricky and Mickey in walking home Mickey's girlfriend, Shelly. We took to the alleys to avoid the attention of the police, who were sure to hassle a group walking the streets after midnight.

My friends referred to the police as "cops," never "officers" like in Holland. There, the only danger came around Tulip Time—the annual Dutch festival—when an unwary person could get beaned by a wooden shoe flying off the foot of a klompen dancer. In Cleveland, the phrase "officer of the law" had taken on a cynical new meaning for me the night Percy the cop wheeled into The Exchange offering "good weed at a reasonable price." He confiscated marijuana from the Fifty-Seventh Street boys and sold it on our block. Although Percy called us "his boys," I trusted him as far as I could throw him—and Percy was a large man. He had little in common with Holland's "Officer Safety," who once spoke to my Cub Scout pack on the topic "How to be safe at home, at school, at play."

Shelly lived deep in Hillbilly Haven, only a mile or so from Ricky's house. But it was far enough to concern me.

In this way I was different from my friends. They were comfortable on the streets—often more so than in their own homes; I didn't like being this far out of my neighborhood. But the night was quiet, and everything was cool.

Rounding the corner of an alley, we smelled the stench rising from the trash bins behind the Pic-N-Pay. Mickey threw a rock with the aim of ringing one of the bins. He missed and nearly hit a passing car.

As we approached Shelly's alley, the same car flew past, almost striking us. In his typical style, Ricky flipped them off and yelled an obscenity. I hated it when Ricky did that. His talking before thinking far too often got us into trouble.

Skidding to a halt, the driver slammed into reverse and brought the car to a stop a few yards from our feet.

He and the passengers jumped out. There were six of them, and they weren't small.

"What you lookin' at?" Ricky yelled, taunting them with clenched fists.

I never felt more alive than I did at that moment when I thought I might soon be dead. I took off my glasses and placed them carefully under some bushes by Shelly's fence, figuring if nothing else, they would remain unbroken.

The assailants got to Ricky first. Then they went for me. Running wasn't an option because I knew if I did, I'd never be able to face my friends again. I fought, but to no avail. I went down hard. That's when I heard the bang.

While Ricky and I were getting pummeled, Mickey had run into Shelly's garage and emerged with a gun. I was partly relieved but mostly terrified. Mickey unloaded the gun into the car that was now racing away.

I managed to get to my feet, but Ricky wasn't moving. Picking him up, we saw blood on his face and neck and a gash on his cheek showing bone. In a small sign of life, Ricky wrapped his bloody fingers around Mickey's head.

Mickey brought Ricky's head to rest on his and wept quietly. I held on to them both, while Shelly went to get help.

An ambulance took Ricky for treatment, and I decided to head home. I was halfway there when I remembered my glasses.

I returned to the alley. The lights were dim, but bright enough for me to see that my glasses were gone. I ran home while thinking up believable scenarios I could tell my parents when they returned the next day.

As I approached the parsonage my heart stopped cold. There was a car in the driveway—my parents had come back early.

I closed my eyes and prayed the driveway empty. But the car remained. Standing in the shadow of the church stairway encasement, I realized time wouldn't change my predicament, so I crept through the narrow walkway between the church and parsonage. My only hope was extinguished when I saw light coming through the drapes of my parents' bedroom window.

Quietly, I entered the front door, aware for the first time of my bloody, bruised body. I tiptoed to the stairway. My father was waiting on the landing, his eyes red and wet. Only once before had I seen water in his eyes—the day he almost lost his finger as he hung from his wedding ring on the edge of a gutter after rescuing my baseball from a rooftop. Unlike then, tonight his tears were a welcome sight. I reached for him and he took me in.

Grace permeated that night. Perhaps most obvious was the grace I experienced in the arms of my father. But grace also permeated a dark, inner-city alley in the bloody embrace of my friends. Despite Ricky's rage that found expression most every minute of every day, and despite Mickey's knack for violence, which had something, if not everything, to do with his mother's leaving and the regular beatings he received from his father, their embrace revealed to me the grace of God.

Cran-Hill Ranch, Michigan, 1971

I awoke thinking the van was a time machine when I saw the beauty of the campground. I felt exhilarated, yet leery of how we would do at a camp that was more for small-town kids than for city dwellers. I didn't know if we could last five minutes in such a place, let alone six days.

The van hadn't come to a full stop before Ben, Mickey, and Ricky jumped out. Ron, our youth worker, yelled, but they were long gone. (Ron was working for AIM, which stood for "Adventure In Mission." He had no idea that his adventure was just beginning.)

I figured they had gone to the pond that we spotted while circling the grounds. Ron looked for traces of their whereabouts while I unloaded the gear and watched other kids arrive. Like white bread out of toasters they popped from their cars, hair neatly combed, summer outfits fresh and clean. They had the latest in luggage, far different from our pile: Ricky's pillow case stuffed with clothes and a dirty old blanket, Mickey's similar belongings, and Ben's brown suitcase, as old as the grandfather who let him use it. A belt held it closed, although a few items saw daylight.

"I've got to find out where they do their shopping," a girl said as she and her friends passed by.

I was glad Ricky wasn't around to hear the comment. If he were, there would have been blood already. Ricky took disparagement from nobody, girls or boys. In fact, he often mouthed off to other people before they could do it to him.

Giving up on finding the boys, Ron walked to the dining hall with me. He figured they would catch up with us sooner or later. I was banking on later.

The camp director was closing dinner with prayer when they arrived. Right through the main dining hall doors they stormed, totally unaware of our spiritual moment.

"Hey Beuk, look at this fat little #&*%!"

I could have crawled under the table. Ricky was holding the frog by its hind legs while poking its belly with a stick. I tried to motion him to be quiet and the others to sit down at the table labeled "Calvary Cleveland." I saw that the director was shooting daggers our way. My fears had been realized.

After a brief message on the week's theme, "In Christ We Have Been Made Friends," the director assigned cabins. Calvary Cleveland had its own cabin. The other church groups had been split up, but as the director said, "We knew you'd like to stay together." He was right. We were as relieved as the kids from the other churches, although I did think that the decision conflicted with theme.

By breakfast the first morning Ricky knew the name of every female in camp, including the women counselors. Diana, the tall, shapely, blonde lifeguard, was number one on Ricky's list. Even though she was a college student with a steady boyfriend, Ricky was confident he would be making out with her by the week's end. I figured it was a long shot but had learned to put nothing past Ricky.

The Sharks, Thunderbirds, Eagles, Dolphins, and Seals made up the teams for the raft contest. Each had a bit of Cleveland, as Uncle Jack, our cabin counselor, insisted the teams not be arranged by cabin. The rafts were to be built from the materials provided near the shore, then raced across the small lake and back. The Thunderbirds won, and Mickey wouldn't shut up about it. Ricky's raft sank, and he wouldn't shut up about it either. He was so angry that he tore apart what remained of the raft with his bare hands. It took the director and two counselors to pull him off the wreckage. We laughed so hard that I thought for a moment we were back at The Exchange.

"Is there anything you guys want to talk about tonight for 'prayer and share'?" Uncle Jack asked on our second evening in the cabin.

"Yeah," said Ricky. "Do you think Diana's a virgin?"

We laughed so hard Uncle Mark from the cabin next door told us to keep it down.

Uncle Jack suggested we talk about sex, since there seemed to be some interest in the subject. Ricky said, "I don't wanna talk about it, I wanna do it!" He jumped off his bedroll and into the middle of the cabin floor, swaying his hips in a junior high mating dance.

Uncle Jack tried not to laugh. I imagine it was his job not to laugh, but he couldn't help it. Then he got serious and told us horsing around like that doesn't bring honor to the subject of sex—that sex is something God created to be a beautiful, loving thing. That's when Ricky interrupted again, this time by jumping on top of Mickey and saying, "Kiss me! It's a beautiful, loving thing!"

Mickey knocked him down hard and swore a streak. This time we just about died laughing. Uncle Jack settled us down and closed the evening with a reading from the Bible and a few last words.

"God doesn't want us having sex outside of a committed relationship," he said. Then he told us a personal story about how kissing his girlfriend had almost led to petting and how he managed to stop in time.

"What's petting?" Ben asked.

"Yeah, what's that? Humpin' your dog?" Ricky joked.

This time the laughter shook the cabin all the way to its foundation. From the cabin next door Uncle Mark screamed for quiet, and Uncle Jack threatened to turn off the light if we didn't get serious. We cooperated so he would keep talking. He explained that sex can only bring honor to God when done in the context of marriage.

This time staying serious, Ricky said, "Well, my ma isn't with my old man. We don't even know where he is. She's got a boyfriend and I hear 'em doin' it all the time, and they ain't married. Uncle Jack, is my ma goin' to hell?"

The cabin went silent. Uncle Jack said that we could talk more about this later. He turned out the light.

Seven o'clock breakfast duty wasn't hard on me, but it was murder on the guys. The rules of the camp were not that different from the rules in my home, where we had set dinner times, chore schedules, homework schedules, and piano practice schedules. My friends had discovered long ago the strangeness of my family, and now they could see where I got it.

While we were setting the table, Diana had every one of Ricky's hormones at full attention. Their back and forth bantering held everyone's interest.

Except for Uncle Mark. "Richard," he said, taking Ricky firmly by the neck, "you are supposed to be setting tables. Now get to it."

I froze, unsure what, if anything, I could do. Uncle Mark, about seven years older and three or four times bigger than Ricky, made the perfect target. I knew there was no way he would expect what was about to happen. He had made two mistakes—he had called him Richard and he had touched him.

Ricky smacked Uncle Mark's hand off his neck and let go a string of curse words. Uncle Mark went to grab him and that's when Ricky hit him square in the face. By the time he even realized what was happening, Ricky had landed at least four more punches.

Blood gushed from his nose. I grabbed Ricky and dragged him toward a nearby tree. Afraid they might send us home, I begged him to cool down.

When Uncle Mark noticed all the blood on his shirt and shoes, he called Ricky a stupid punk. Diana and another counselor restrained Uncle Mark, while Mickey and Ben helped me hold onto Ricky.

The director entered the confusion and asked what was going on. Ricky explained his side of things, in words that were mostly vulgar. After Uncle Mark screamed out his defense, the director told us to take Ricky back to the cabin. In the cabin we convinced Ricky that Uncle Mark obviously had emotional problems and that he should let it go. Ricky let it go and fortunately so did the director.

We enjoyed the afternoons more than any other part of the day. Horseback riding, archery, tetherball, basketball, and swimming held our attention in ways far different from Cleveland's streets.

The camp was another world and I could see its peace claim a hold on my friends. I saw it on Ricky's face the day his horse decided to make his own trail despite Ricky's best efforts. I saw it on Mickey's face when at the archery range he watched his arrow disappear into a cloud. I heard it in Ben's voice during "prayer and share" when he included every minute detail of his hike to the pond, where he caught over thirty frogs, chased chipmunks, and saw a fawn. And I noticed a certain lightness in my own gait that had been missing for some time.

The last night around a campfire was when all the campers were asked to follow Jesus. Before agreeing to follow him, Ricky wanted to know where Jesus was going. I thought it was a good question, but the director didn't seem to understand Ricky's serious side. It was, in fact, the only side Ricky had.

During our cabin's last "prayer and share," we felt the sadness of having to leave. Ricky didn't cry, but he came close, which I figured fell just short of the miracle of the Feeding of the Five Thousand that we had talked about earlier that week. During our closing prayer, Ben thanked God for the fawns and frogs. Mickey thanked God for letting his team win the boat race. Ricky thanked God for Uncle Jack. I thanked God for all the new friends we had made. We all said amen.

We liked having Uncle Jack as our cabin counselor, not only because he tried hard to understand us, but also because he was a heavy sleeper. Every night he was out cold by eleven o'clock, allowing us to sneak off to a wooded area near the lavatories. The place was well covered by trees and brush, yet allowed visual access for monitoring counselor activity. The first night the congregants were all from Cleveland, but by the last night there were Jill and Cathy from Kalamazoo, Ricky's girlfriend Janet from Grandville, two of her friends from Grand Rapids, three girls from Muskegon (one of whom had made fun of our luggage that first day), Carl (a preacher's kid from Canada), and two of his friends. Carl brought a bottle of wine. Our time together was quiet and close. For a while we reminisced. And then we toasted the week. It was the second service of communion we shared that night.

The next morning we passed through the gates and under the sign that read, "In Christ we have been made friends."

Chicago, 1998

I told C. J. before my students arrived that I didn't expect him to talk about it. But during the session a student asked him about the gang activity in the neighborhood, and I guess he just couldn't let it go.

He was ten years old when he buckled under the pressure. "They slammed me against the school yard fence and wouldn't take no for an answer," he said. He explained that if he valued his health, there was nothing he could do except agree to the arrangement. Selling the packets would be easy with all the product demand and income of one hundred dollars a day would keep him and his brothers in Air Jordan sneakers and his family in food.

"Besides," he explained, "all my friends were hooked-up. I had no choice."

A few of the customers were local, but most drove in from the suburbs with their fancy cars and thick wallets.

C. J. was one of the many runners. He explained the pyramid structure—a general at the top followed by lieutenants, corporals, sergeants, and on down to the runners—each receiving a piece of the take. Like most any business, the real power and profit was in the hands of the few at the top.

C. J.'s arrangements with the gang were ironclad. Although he would never have to worry about the financial well-being of his family, he also knew there was only one way out.

"Taking a bullet. That's the only way," he explained. "Not my idea of an attractive retirement package."

He was close to the top when he decided to get out. "I guess I just popped one too many," he said, referring to his responsibilities as head of the security council. He estimated that somewhere between twenty and thirty young men had lost their lives from the twitch of his finger.

"I was dead anyway. Taking a bullet was the best way out."

The time for the termination ritual was set. The place would be the same where six years earlier C. J. was inducted, a ritual in which the inductee is led into the "holy circle" and pummeled non-stop for thirty minutes by fellow gang members. Now the General ordered the Second Lieutenant of Arms to take his position behind the kneeling C. J. The lieutenant's pistol was drawn. The members offered their prayer in unison, "You are dust and to dust you shall return." As C. J. described it, "the presence of God filled the night."

When the cold steel of the pistol touched the base of his skull, C. J. looked to his friends as if to say, "It's okay, man. It's okay." Then the Second Lieutenant of Arms dropped the pistol to the ground and explained to the

General that he couldn't carry out the order and would accept the mandated disciplinary action of the council. The General then called in another.

"I knew it was all over when he called Sherita to take up arms. Let's just say things didn't end too well with us a few years back. I figured she was just waiting to put a bullet in my head," C. J. explained.

Sherita touched the barrel to C. J.'s head and the community prayers continued. Seconds later the gun once again found the ground as Sherita ran out from the circle.

"You see," C. J. explained, "we live for each other and we die for each other. But justice had to be done, and so the General said he'd do it himself. He lifted the pistol and I heard a click. The seconds seemed like hours. And then he pushed me down and told me to leave their holy land and never return. I left for a few years but when my mother took ill I had to come back. But things are cool now. They pretty much leave me alone."

My students were dumbstruck. Finally, a student asked C. J. the obvious: "Why did they let you go?" C. J. smiled. "They love me, man."

Some readers may find it a stretch to consider that boys like Ricky and Mickey, or men like C. J., bear the image of God. But I have found God in unexpected places on more than a few occasions.

The Scriptures bear witness to the grace common to all humans. Unfortunately the church, like the Pharisees of Jesus' day, has a tendency to exclude some of God's children from a table that has been set for all. The church would be wise to remember that on many occasions in the Bible God turns his face away from those marked with a grace considered special, in favor of those considered most common or unholy. In the Old Testament, God surprises

Israel by using such men, women, and nations to fulfill his purposes. In the New Testament we encounter the same God when we find Jesus with the woman at the well and at the table with tax collectors. We can learn to expect the unexpected when it comes to encountering God's grace.

CHAPTER 5

Evangelism

*The Spirit of the Lord is upon me, because he has
anointed me to bring good news to the poor. He
has sent me to proclaim release to the captives and
recovery of sight to the blind, to let the oppressed
go free, to proclaim the year of the Lord's favor.*
—Luke 4:18-19

Cleveland, 1966

I observed my neighborhood from my bedroom window my first summer in Cleveland. The action on Sixty-Fifth Street would set off my imagination for hours.

I was fascinated by the men and women who stopped at our front door with hopes for some food or loose change. Located between two main avenues, the parsonage provided a pit stop of sorts for the large number of transients on their way to the trash bins behind local restaurants. There the down and out could find fresh scraps of food thrown away daily by establishments whose front doors they couldn't afford to enter.

It was on one of our first summer days when my mother yelled from the kitchen, "What happened to the bread and the lunch meat?"

I walked slowly into the kitchen. When she raised my chin to meet her eyes, I confessed, "They came to the door and asked if we had some food. I fixed them some sandwiches." Drawing me close, my mother let out a sound somewhere between a cry and a laugh.

The families moving into our neighborhood were primarily from West Virginia and Kentucky. Cars and station wagons packed with mothers, children, and household belongings filled our church parking lot, which served as a temporary stopping place while fathers hunted for the few jobs in Cleveland's factories.

My father called it our parking lot ministry. I was put in charge of sandwiches.

Cleveland, 1967

That winter my father devised a plan to put new shoes on the feet of neighborhood children. Pulling my wagon, I walked with him up and down Loraine and Detroit Avenues, where shops of shoe and clothing merchants lined the streets.

Within a week the church basement was stacked with brand new shoes. The church had found a way into the lives of the merchants, and the merchants had found a way into the life of the church.

Together we called it our shoe ministry. I was put in charge of transportation.

Cleveland, Christmas 1969

The pounding intruded upon my dream. I awoke in a panic, thinking I had overslept. It was Christmas morning, but I couldn't be late delivering papers to my 105 holiday customers.

I looked at the alarm clock—only 3:00 a.m. I relaxed and prepared to go back to sleep. Then I heard the pounding again and realized it hadn't been a dream. I fumbled for my glasses, threw on my pants, and rushed down the stairs, taking them two at a time.

In a matter of seconds, my father was up shouting evacuation orders. Soon we were standing across the street, watching the fire.

The parsonage roof was smoking, and the church was in flames. The stained glass was popping and the lead melting.

Fire trucks swarmed. I observed my father scurrying around the scene. He talked to the fire chief, hunted for keys and information, scrutinized the strategies of the fighters, and did all that he was allowed to do—very little. Around six o'clock in the morning, the church fell down.

Dawn broke on the ruins, and on the gathering that had assembled during the night. I saw Mr. Lenart. His eyes were teary.

I thought this was strange. Mr. Lenart hardly seemed a man of faith. Just a few weeks earlier, my father and I had watched from our front porch as he emptied a gun into a passing car. Later we learned it was in retaliation for the load of buckshot the car's passengers had fired through his windows. Yet his tears this morning did not seem those of an ungodly man.

Looking around, I saw that many other people had tears—church and non-church people alike. I said to my mother, "I think the neighborhood is crying."

The grief that morning showed the connection of the church to its local community. Attendance had risen dramatically—families of all kinds now filled Calvary's pews on Sunday mornings. A ministry that began with a bicycle giveaway, a parking lot respite for families in transition, and a shoe distribution program had grown to include a food co-op, music instruction, an emergency food pantry, a weekly lunch program for seniors, youth programs, and legal assistance. Although the preached Word never lost its central place at Calvary, my father would often say, "The gospel must be proclaimed in its fullness, and that means every day of the week."

It was around this time when I first noticed changes in my father. In particular, he talked differently. Words like *fairness, justice,* and *peace* found their way into the sermon titles he posted on the announcement board on the church lawn.

Not long before the fire, I even heard my father swear. It happened while driving home from a denominational meeting, at which he had tried to explain to his non-urban colleagues why the gospel is relevant to matters such as economics, jobs, and health care. His was a lonely place.

Only two things were salvaged from the ruins of the fire: the cross that had stood behind the pulpit and the Good Shepherd stained glass window. Scorched by the blaze, the cross of solid oak had turned an ash black. It was beautiful. Its survival amazed everyone.

The survival of the Good Shepherd window was no less miraculous. The other stained glass windows had broken apart into their component pieces, as the fire melted the lead that held them together. Although in need of some repair, the image of Jesus as the Good Shepherd remained in remarkable condition. It was difficult to extricate from among the frozen pews, fixtures, and other church remains, but my father spared no expense to rescue the window from the rubble.

It hurt to see the empty space left by the fire, but the time for sorrow was short. Soon after the fire my father announced a building campaign he called "Building Hope In The City." It was as though we had moved from the pain of Good Friday to the joy of Easter morning in a few months.

The idea of a new building created excitement in the neighborhood. As I learned more fully years later, through a building project in Chicago, the urban poor view land as a spiritual matter. For those who are landless, a piece of property is a sign of well-being. (I once found myself in an argument with a denominational executive who wanted to launch a "house church" model of church development in the city. My point was simple: a house church makes sense in the suburbs, where Christians are "land rich," not in the city, where people are "land poor.")

Of course, at the time of the fire in Cleveland, I had my own reasons for desiring a new church facility. The Sunday worship crowd in the parsonage had found its way into our kitchen and up the stairway, and was inching ever closer to my bedroom.

While most people had the Apollo space program on their minds, the space that interested me was what little I had left of my own. Such is the life of a preacher's kid.

Chicago, 1996

A few members of the Church of the Good News spoke to a group of seminarians on the theme of community ministry. The following excerpts are from the taped session:

There's this church in Indiana. They send buses into our community to pick up our children and take them to their church. . . . Anyway, last summer they came into our community on a Saturday and set up a stage and sound system to put on a concert while they witnessed to the kids and parents gathered around. At first I thought this was really cool, be-

cause the people of our community need Jesus as
much as the people of any neighborhood. But then I
started thinking, trying to figure out why this was
bothering me.

And then a man from the Indiana church approached me. I listened to his testimony and then
told him that I believe in Jesus and belong to the
Church of the Good News. But he kept witnessing
anyway. Finally I stopped him and said, "Can I ask
you a question?" He said, "Sure."

I said, "This is really nice that you come here to
do this, but I'm just wondering, Where are you
going to be tomorrow and Monday and Tuesday?
You see that little boy over there? He was cornered
a few weeks ago by some gangbangers. They told
him that if he doesn't sell drugs for them, they're
going to beat him up—bad. My neighbors and I
take turns walking him to and from school. . . .

"Do you see that woman over there you were
just talking to? Do you know she's a cocaine addict?
Puts all her money up her nose. We're trying to get
her some help. You guys come here one or two days
a summer, but these people need Jesus every day!"
—*Sharon*

When I was a kid I used to run into Good News
when it was in the storefront on George Street. I'd
run in, mess with Liala, then run out. One evening I
was gonna go to a party. I said, "I can't go to the
party, I gotta go to church!" So I went to Good
News, but I also went to other churches—Baptist
churches—churches that would sing, you know? I
mean, if the church ain't singin', I figure I'm not in
church! Then Liala says we're gonna have a choir. I

said, "Alright!" And she said it's gonna be a community choir and that you don't have to be a member of the church to sing in it. I said, "Great!" because I wasn't ready to be a member.

I tried singing in other church choirs, but there was always arguing goin' on. Everyone was concerned about who was gonna sing this, or who was gonna sing that. . . . So I started goin' to Good News more and more. A couple months ago I joined the church. . . .

I'm not gonna lead any Bible studies like Sharon—that's just not my gift. But I am helping to start a food co-op in our neighborhood. The food pantry's okay, but it makes people feel ashamed—standin' in a line like pigs at a trough. So we're gonna buy a bunch of food cheap so folks can come, volunteer some time, and get a discount on some *good* food.

Of course, a lot of people are gonna want the food and they ain't gonna want to work for it. So they've got some learnin' to do because I'm gonna be running this show. . . . And I know everybody. Ain't nobody gonna pull nothin' over my eyes.
—*Zsame*

I moved into the neighborhood a few years ago. Being disabled —well, I'm HIV positive—I was unable to hold a job and I needed to do something with my time. My involvement with Good News started when Liala asked for my help in carrying some books and items to the church. . . . I told her that if she ever needed any more help at the church—answering phones, washing windows, or whatever—I'd be happy to help out. Last summer the challenge came when she asked me to teach in the summer Bible school program. I said, "Now wait a minute—I don't know that I can handle kids!" You see, I don't have children of my own. . . . Besides, although I was raised in a church, I really didn't know much of anything about the Bible. But, boy, did I learn! I'd come over to Liala and George's house just about every night with all my questions.

The week of Bible school was the most rewarding week of my life. Seeing those children look up to me, asking me questions, and just inviting me into their lives was overwhelming. Since then I've become a member and am very involved in the community. You can't be in this church and not be involved in the community. I'm on the board of the Lathrop Community Music Center, I'm involved in the choir, and I help our neighborhood organize around issues that are important to our people.

I'd like to tell you a little about the community issues group. It all started when I was at a community meeting and someone said that some big businessman who owns a building down the street from the church, right across from Lathrop, was going to rent some space to a pawnshop. Well, you know what that means! [Pawnshops encourage theft as they provide cash for goods with few, if any, questions asked.] Boy, did this news create a stir! We called a special community meeting and decided we didn't want a pawnshop in our neighborhood. . . .

So we made a plan. First, we appointed a small group of us to meet with the building owner and see if we could convince him to rent the space for another purpose—something that would help the community, not hurt it. Well, his secretary kept telling us that he was too busy. So then we decided to visit him anyway—just to let him know that we weren't going away!

So about fifteen of us piled into the church van and went to his business office. Very politely we waited in the lobby until he finally agreed to see us. He listened to our concerns but told us that he could rent the space in his building to anyone he wanted, and that the owner of the pawnshop had every right to do business wherever he wanted. "It's a free country," he said. Then Pastor Liala said, "But don't you think you have some responsibility to our community? Doesn't freedom involve responsibility?" That was a good one! Anyway, he got mad and told us to leave him alone.

So we went back to the church and held another meeting. We decided we would go to city hall and talk to Mayor Daley. This time we brought two vanloads of people! We didn't get to talk to the mayor, but we did talk to one of his aides. About a week later, Pastor Liala got a call from the building owner saying that he changed his mind. He decided not to rent to the pawnshop. Man did we have a party. . . .

Jim, the owner of a small business in our neighborhood, had joined our effort because he knew a pawnshop would hurt his business. Anyway, a couple of weeks later at a job rally, Jim asks me, "Why does your church do this kind of stuff? I thought churches do Bible studies and things like that." I told him that we do a lot of that. I told him that it's the Bible that teaches *our* community is *God's* community. And the way we figure it, God doesn't want a pawnshop in his neighborhood either! —*Ray*

I've been associated with the Church of the Good News since its inception. My family was one of the first black families to move into Lathrop Homes. This church has always been an integral part of the community. We have black folk, Hispanic folk, white folk, and all kinds of folk! And you don't have to be a member to belong here. People who've never attended a service claim this church as their church. Just a few months ago a young boy was killed. His mother asked to have the funeral here. Over three hundred people squeezed into our sanctuary for the funeral. That's just the way it is here.

And when we built the new building, we didn't just make our own plans. We asked folks in the community for input. We ended up changing the whole design after talking to the people from the Head Start daycare program. We decided it would be great to have them in our building, but the city codes for a daycare facility were very strict. It was more expensive to build it this way, but it was worth it. Every weekday we have sixty kids and their parents walking in and out of this church. . . .

That leads me to tell you about the Lathrop Community Music Center, which is also in our building. About twelve years ago we had this idea. It was around the time our President was saying things like, "Say no to drugs." Well, that's easy for him to say! The problem is that our kids have little to say yes to. Did you know that there's not one teacher in our neighborhood school that can play an instrument? Can you believe that? That's terrible!

So George asked me, and some community folk, to check out a place in Uptown called the People's Music Center. They have over a hundred and fifty children and adults taking music lessons—a half-hour a week of private instruction and an hour each week of theory instruction. They have some of Chicago's best musicians teaching for less than half the going rate. Some even do it for free!

We visited the school during a recital, and we saw children, teenagers, mothers, fathers, and grandparents performing on stage. You should have seen the look on their faces—concentrating—focusing—determined to make their loved ones proud. In the van on the way home from our visit we decided to start our own music center!

The next Saturday morning we met at the church, drew up some flyers, then scattered them throughout the neighborhood. The message was simple: "Interested in playing a musical instrument? If so, come to the Church of the Good News at one o'clock this afternoon." We figured if people didn't come, then it wasn't a good idea and we should be doing something else.

But by the time one o'clock came around, we had a church crammed with people! Today we have a board of directors, a full-time executive director, over ten quality musicians on staff, and over one hundred students! —*Maynard*

Starting the Lathrop Community Music Center was exciting but not without its challenges—one of which was raising money. I received a phone call from a large, affluent congregation in a nearby suburb. They had heard about the music program and were considering funding a portion of the ministry.

They sent a group of men from their mission committee to spend a day with me to learn about the church, the community, and the music program. The men seemed pleased with the day's activities, particularly their conversations with the young people involved in the music program.

The next day I received a phone call from the committee chair. He explained that they wanted to support the ministry, but their support hinged on one condition. They had noticed that the music teachers didn't begin their lessons with prayer. The chairman said that if the teachers would agree to pray with their students before each lesson, they would contribute five thousand dollars to the program; if not, they would direct their money elsewhere.

I explained that the philosophy of the music center is to communicate God's love through his gift of music in the context of caring relationships. I assured him that the members of our church pray constantly for the music center, its teachers, and its students. I also explained that while our music teachers are required to be fine musicians, they are not required to be Christians (although most are). We want to be a witness to both students and teachers. He said that he was sorry; the money would have to go toward a more Christian program.

Some readers may argue that this chapter should have been titled "Social Action" rather than "Evangelism." I would disagree. To name it so would validate the notion that word and deed can be separated—a dualism that has plagued the church for centuries.

Both the words and deeds of Christians proclaim the good news of Jesus Christ. God utters a word, and the earth is formed; Israel trumpets a cry, and the walls of Jericho fall down. A spoken word is a living deed. Likewise, a deed is a living word. On many occasions Jesus acts rather than speaks his words. For example, Jesus is virtually silent about his impending crucifixion, yet his assent to the cross speaks volumes.

The connection between word and deed reflects the mystery of the incarnation, the Living Word that is Jesus Christ. If Christians desire to evangelize their community, they must proclaim living words and living deeds. But such action can only happen as Christians become one with the community. They must share in its life, its joy, and its suffering. If Christians desire to evangelize their community, they must seek to be its Living Word.

CHAPTER 6

Righteous Anger

*O Lord, how long shall I cry for help, and you will
not listen? Or cry to you "Violence!" and you will
not save? Why do you make me see wrongdoing
and look at trouble? Destruction and violence are
before me; strife and contention arise. So the law
becomes slack and justice never prevails.*
—Habakkuk 1:2-4a

Cleveland, 1967

The principal of the neighborhood school asked my
father to visit a family that had recently arrived from
Guatemala. The children had a poor attendance record,
and the principal was concerned.

Receiving no response from his knocks, my father
started to leave. Then the doorknob wiggled and the door
opened just a crack. The mother's face poked out. My father smiled and greeted her.

Perhaps it was the sight of my father's collar that
brought tears to her eyes. She opened the door and let
him in.

Her six children were huddled in the center of the
small kitchen. Rags and towels were sticking out of the

cracks and crevices of the windows and doorways. The oven door hung open, and the smell of gas permeated the room. If my father had visited an hour or two later, it is likely the mother's attempt to kill herself and her family would have been successful.

Their trip to the States had taken all of their resources. Their food supply was depleted, and eviction from their apartment was imminent. The mother had minimal English skills, which prevented her from getting the government assistance that was available to her. The reason for the children's poor school attendance was quite simple—they took turns using the one pair of shoes the family owned.

Cleveland, 1969

I was at Ben's house watching television with him and his little brother when a man stormed through the kitchen door. In a flash, Ben took off up the stairs and Ben's little brother crawled behind the sofa.

Swearing a blue streak, the man stumbled into the living room. When he saw me, he froze, then continued his rampage.

Ben came down the stairs with a baseball bat in his hand. The man asked where Ben's mother was. Ben said he didn't know.

He told Ben to put the bat down. Ben refused. The man lunged, ripped it away from him, and threw it against the wall. He smacked Ben with an open hand that sent him to the floor.

Ben's little brother ran out the front door. I tried to follow but was paralyzed with fear.

The man entered the kitchen, shouting curses and tossing kitchen items. He came back into the room with a kitchen knife in his hand. It was then that my father walked through the front door, shadowed by Ben's little brother.

My father asked the man to put down the knife. The man said a Reverend had no business sticking his nose where it didn't belong. My father explained it *was* his business and again asked him to put down the knife.

The man dropped the weapon and collapsed on the floor. Ben ran out the door.

I found Ben sitting on the loading dock down at the Exchange. He told me he was going to kill his old man. It was then that I realized I had just met Ben's father.

Ben told me that my father was crazy for stepping in the way he did. I had to agree.

Cleveland, 1973

Turning at the sound of someone calling me, I saw a boy I didn't recognize. I continued my walk home from school. He called out again. The voice sounded familiar, so I turned and walked toward him.

The group darted out from behind a house, and before I knew what was happening there were about eight guys over me. I lifted my head in an attempt to summon anyone within earshot, and a boot struck my face.

When my eyes regained their focus, I saw a pool of blood that had gathered in a bald spot in the grass. Pushing myself to my feet, I saw a man and woman standing nearby. It was their lawn that I had stained. I asked them for help, but they wouldn't move a muscle. Spitting out bloody words, I staggered toward home.

I awoke among voices, bright lights, and busy hands. My eyes wandered until they reached the soft eyes of what appeared to be an Asian angel in white.

I awoke again, seeing nothing but the minute threads of a piece of fabric draped over my face. I felt tug after tug on what I assumed was my face, but what felt more like a piece of loosely attached leather.

When I awoke again, my father had hold of my hand. My ears took in his words of assurance: "You are going to be all right."

In the recovery room my father asked me what had happened. My head still scrambled, I had to give the question back to him. He told me that Ben had found me in a neighbor's yard and helped me to the parsonage. Sherry, the youth worker, rushed me to Mercy General.

My father explained the surgeon's handiwork. He said that the white stitches placed on the inside of my mouth would dissolve in a week's time and that the black ones placed on the outside would be removed in a week or two. He asked me how I felt. I told him they had good drugs at Mercy General.

The police visited later that day.

"Who did this to you?" the one with glasses asked.

"Probably some gang punks," said the heavy one, while jotting something down in his notebook.

"Listen," the officer said, looking to my father. "We'll make a report, but I'm going to tell you the truth here. Our philosophy's quite simple when it comes to these punks. We just let them kill each other off."

Irate, my father made it clear that I was not one of those punks. The interview was over and they left the room.

I told my father that it wasn't fair. He agreed, saying I didn't deserve what happened to me. But he didn't understand what I meant and I was too drowsy to explain.

Having a prayer chapel in the new church was my father's idea. The chapel was where the Good Shepherd window from the remains of the old church had found its new home.

I liked the room and often enjoyed its quiet. But the day I returned from the hospital, I had a different agenda with the Good Shepherd. His gentle smile triggered what had been building up over the years.

I was angry. I was angry with the boys who split open my face. I was angry with my friends for retaliating the next day and putting two of my assailants in the hospital. I was angry that my neighborhood was in such a mess. I was angry that the city was in such a mess.

I was angry that a mother could find herself in such despair that she would choose to take the lives of her children. I was angry that some boys on Fifty-Seventh Street could be so dead inside that they would stuff a small black boy into a garbage can and burn him alive.

I was angry with parents who couldn't, or wouldn't, take care of themselves. I was angry that little children had to take care of themselves. I was angry that the police sold drugs to my friends one minute and the next called them punks. I was angry that so many fathers couldn't find work to support their families. I was angry at the factories that moved South so they could reap larger profits at the expense of city jobs.

I was angry with people who didn't seem to care. I was angry with people who had so much while so many had so little.

I was angry that I was so angry. I was angry that no one else seemed angry.

I approached the Good Shepherd and screamed.

Chicago, 1985

She saw more clearly than most sighted people. Her "Bible with bumps," as the Good News children called it, kept her fingers busy much of each day, and her wit and wisdom added a great stone to the church's foundation.

If Peter was a rock, Corrine was a boulder. Her personal story remains mostly unknown, because she spoke little of herself. Yet her almost daily presence in the church provided hope and encouragement to the many who entered its doors.

I inherited Corrine along with the rest of the Sonshine Club, a group of Lathrop's elderly who had little in the way of money or family. Quite simply, the club provided them a reason to get out of bed each morning.

Thursday was shopping day. Knowing Corrine required little food, I was mystified at her overflowing grocery bags. I imagined her Lathrop apartment packed with supplies worthy of a disaster relief bunker, but when a visit to her home revealed cupboards mostly bare, I thought perhaps Corrine had a higher than normal metabolism.

A visit with her neighbor Eileen cleared up the mystery. There I discovered a pantry full of items from Corrine's weekly shopping trips. Eileen told of Corrine's food ministry to the many families of her building.

The wind was biting on the February night I got the phone call. The concern rose from a neighbor's unanswered knocks on Corrine's door. (Matching, if not surpassing, the horrors of life in public housing is the daily care one receives in most any building in Lathrop.)

Rousing the building captain from her sleep, I borrowed the key to Corrine's apartment. Inside, I could see my breath as if I were still outdoors, due to the cold radiators and the wind passing through the cracks in the walls around the windows.

I found her slouched in the only chair, loosely wrapped in a blanket no thicker than the flannel shirt under my parka. Wrapping her in a comforter offered by a neighbor, I carried her to the apartment of another neighbor fortunate enough to have heat. Intense rubbing warmed her flesh while we waited an hour for the paramedics to arrive.

"Should have taken her to your home, Reverend. Would have been well cared for by now," the neighbor said, voicing what was obvious to everyone in the apartment but me.

Although I lived only a block away, I did not live in the "projects," where excuses like fear of gangs and muggings are too familiar to the residents.

The paramedics' examination was brief. Upon finding a healthy heartbeat, reasonable blood pressure, and no signs of frostbite, the paramedics quickly left the premises.

Perhaps warm radiator pipes would have been a blessing. But I had learned the folly of believing the obvious. Warm pipes may have kept Corrine well, but doctors and nurses who work the burn unit at the local hospital would attest to the harm they do to Lathrop's children. When the apartments were remodeled in the early sixties, cost-cutting dictated that the radiator pipes be placed outside the new walls and a few inches above the floorboards. Parents did what they could to cover the hot pipes, but their efforts couldn't counter the curiosity and tenacity of normal children at play.

Good windows would have been a blessing. Here again the remodelers had opted for a quick and cheap approach. The remodeling crews had left the windows and surrounding tuck-pointing completely untouched. Within months the newly installed walls and ceilings were growing mildew from weather that couldn't be kept outside.

If the segregation of the poor in Cleveland brought its challenges, I came to learn the deeper ills of a public housing system that stacks poor on top of poor and implements policies that keep them in exactly that position.

Originally a beautiful development in a location that pro-voked the envy of Chicago's other public housing com-munities, Lathrop went downhill fast when the concerns of the residents lost their place in the management process.

There was a time when the people took pride in their community. There was a time when a child from a poor family in Lathrop could expect to see a neighbor come home after a good day's work at one of the nearby facto-ries, businesses, or hospitals. There was a time when, if a child was caught destroying housing property, the family would be warned, and if the offense was repeated, evicted. There was a time when every candidate for residency went through a screening procedure, including a thorough background check.

There was a time of gardens beautifully kept, stair-ways cleaned and cleared, garbage put in proper contain-ers—a time when people were grateful to have quality, af-fordable housing while they pursued an education or searched for a living-wage job. There was a time when housing policies were designed with the input of residents.

Times changed. Perhaps most devastating was the pol-icy fixing the rental fee at about one-third of a resident's income. It no longer made economic sense for a family above the poverty line to live in Lathrop. Economically stable families moved out of the community.

This policy also left the remaining residents trapped. Because most financial advisors counsel families against spending more than twenty-five percent of their income on housing—and banks rarely grant mortgages to persons in such situations—the policy assured that few, if any, Lathrop residents, would ever be in a position to leave.

While harmful policies were created, beneficial ones, like the required screening of tenant applicants were abandoned. Residents who wanted a healthy and safe community for their children found themselves overwhelmed with deeply troubled families and individuals lacking supportive resources. Little by little, the residents lost control of their community. Their understanding of Lathrop's problems, and their wisdom concerning its solutions, were ignored. Decisions were made by a system blind to their humanity.

If you wonder why some urban poor people seem apathetic about their communities, consider a crushed spirit. If you wonder why urban ministers are often angry, consider the experiences of the boy screaming at the Good Shepherd. If you wonder why urban congregations spend so much time and energy fighting for things like fair policies, living-wage jobs, and safe and affordable housing, consider Corrine. And if you wonder if there's a biblical precedent for righteous anger, consider Habakkuk.

CHAPTER 7

Sin

For our struggle is not against human foes, but against cosmic powers, against the authorities and potentates of this dark world, against the superhuman forces of evil in the heavens.
—Ephesians 6:12, NEB

Cleveland, 1970

The Shalom Singers probably saved my life. Formed primarily to bring the energy of youth more fully into the worship experience, the Shalom Singers provided my friends and me a safe alternative to Cleveland's streets. Strenuous practice, matching outfits, and numerous road trips brought cohesion and purpose to the group.

While insurance money provided some of the funds for building a new church facility after the fire, the Shalom Singers made their contribution by performing concerts at churches in western Michigan—the "breadbasket" of our denomination. Testimonies through song and story brought tears to countless mothers, fathers, and children, as well as the much-needed offerings.

Sleeping at the homes of members of host congregations was not a matter of choice. Although we often begged for permission to stay together in the host church's building, we were split into groups in the interest of building relationships.

To say that this provided families with an interesting cross-cultural experience would be an understatement. I recall one visit quite well. I was paired with Ben.

"Okay, now I need two boys to go with the Postmas," said the host pastor.

"George and Ben, get your things," my father directed.

I remember the look of disappointment on Mr. Postma's face. Drawing one of the minister's kids was not what he had bargained for. But he didn't know that Ben would more than make up for it.

We drove to the Postmas' house in their brand new white Cadillac. Ben never stopped playing with the automatic windows.

"Come on in boys," Mrs. Postma said, motioning us toward the front door of their suburban palace.

Ben was quick to give them his yarn about his family and neighborhood—stories mostly true, but never told as straight as an arrow. It always worked. In minutes, he'd be offered most anything in the house.

But I couldn't blame Ben for his manipulative tactics. As I figured it, he was fourteen going on thirty and deserved a little, if not a lot, of spoiling. Besides, it put families like the Postmas in their glory.

"Got any good sh__ to eat?" Ben said, his language guard not quite high enough.

Mrs. Postma stammered. She finally got out the words: "Yes, you must be famished. I'll fix you boys something while Hank shows you around."

Looking out the picture window, Ben asked Mr. Postma about the park's pool hours, noticing it stood empty. Mr. Postma explained that it wasn't a community pool, but one he had built for his grandson, and that it wasn't a park, but his backyard.

Mr. Postma directed us to the basement. I knew what to expect, although it took Ben by surprise. A finely finished recreation room, the basement was equipped with a pool table, Ping-Pong table, color television set, and all sorts of games.

"You boys can come down and play after you get something in your stomachs," Mr. Postma said.

But I don't think Ben heard him. He was dumbfounded by all the options before him. When we entered the living room, Ben expressed his true feelings, "Holy sh__! This room is bigger than my whole house!" It was either Ben's language or a sense of guilt that sent Mr. and Mrs. Postma scurrying off to the kitchen for the platter of food.

Later in the evening Ben asked the Postmas how they managed to get all their "cool stuff." He intended no disrespect or negative judgment; he was simply trying to understand something he had never experienced.

After some pause, Mrs. Postma said, "God has really blessed us, Ben."

"Yes, God has been very good," Mr. Postma echoed.

I couldn't help but wonder what my family had done wrong!

If the Postmas' explanation bothered me, I could only imagine what it did to Ben. If God had been so good to them, why had he been so bad to Ben's family, and Ricky's, and Gina's, and Debbie's? What mortal sins had they committed? I decided there had to be another explanation for why some have so much and others so little. It didn't seem right. And I could tell that it seemed wrong to the Postmas too. They couldn't hide their discomfort, at least not with Ben in the house.

There were reasons for the economic inequities between the people of these churches and the people of my neighborhood—about this I was certain. But only later did I realize how complicated and emotionally charged the topic of poverty was.

Conversations around such matters seemed to bring out the worst in people. For hours on end, my Hope College classmates and I would argue about who is to blame for economic inequities in our country and world. My classmates claimed the problem lay with the likes of Ben, who were either too lazy or too stupid to change their economic predicament. I knew this wasn't true. My Cleveland friends were among the hardest working people I had ever known. Granted, some of their economic activity was of the illegal kind, but to say that they lacked initiative was ludicrous.

To say they lacked intelligence was also untrue. Most mothers on public assistance could make a dollar stretch farther than the most Dutch of Dutchmen. (Being of Dutch extraction, I know this comment extends a compliment, not an insult, to the Dutch.)

I came to believe the blame for the disparity between rich and poor belonged at the feet of the wealthy and powerful—those who have much and seem always to want more. More recently, however, I see that while the greed of individuals is part of the problem, our economic system, coupled with a distorted belief system, is at the heart of the problem. As the apostle Paul states, our struggle is against not ordinary human enemies but cosmic powers, authorities, potentates, and superhuman forces of evil.

Minnesota, 1990

An elder of a church in rural Minnesota gave me an education when he drove me from the Sioux Falls airport to the church where I was to speak. Perhaps wanting a preview of my presentation on "The Promises and Perils of Urban Ministry," he asked me to name the biggest obstacle facing the people of my community.

"Living-wage jobs," I said.

"I wouldn't have guessed that," he replied. "I was sure you'd say gangs or drugs."

I explained that these were serious problems in our community but symptomatic of deeper ills. After some thought he said, "Jobs may be our biggest problem as well."

He explained that many farms in his community had gone bankrupt over the last number of years. The farmers borrowed too much money in an attempt to compete with the large, corporate farms. He told of the young people in his congregation who were being forced to take jobs in neighboring factories, even though many of them would like nothing more than to work the family farm.

Soon our conversation turned toward the government. "It's a frustrating thing for a farmer," he said, trying to explain to me, a naive city boy, a government crop subsidy program.

"You mean the government pays a farmer for *not* growing crops?" I asked.

"Basically," he responded.

"Oh, sort of like welfare then?" (If looks could kill, I would have been dead!)

"What I mean," I quickly added, "is that it sounds like the situation of many of the people in my neighborhood. They want nothing more than a decent job with a decent wage. Many will do most anything to get off the welfare rolls, but if a job pays only minimum wage and doesn't offer benefits, they can't afford to get off the public aid system."

I told him about Gladys. The words she spoke to a visiting church group describe her situation well.

I really don't like being on welfare. I've always wanted to work. There are some people in Lathrop who don't want to work, but most of us do. Well, I heard about a job at a box factory down the street. I applied and I couldn't believe it, I got the job! I was so excited!

The next Sunday I came to church and shared the good news with everyone during prayer time. It's not the best job in the world, just folding boxes, but the boxes are being made to ship Christian books. I felt like I was really working for the Lord!

Everything was fine until a few weeks ago. My little girl, Cheryl, is a bleeder. When she gets a nosebleed I have to take her to the hospital because it just won't stop. She used to get these a lot, but lately it's been getting better. I was just praying that she wouldn't get sick anymore because when I took the job I had to give up my green card.

"What's a 'green card'?" asked a Wisconsin youth.

"A green card provides health insurance, " Gladys explained. "But you have to give it up when you get a job." She continued,

Since my job didn't provide benefits, I knew I'd be in trouble if Cheryl got sick again. But I decided to risk it. Well, a couple of weeks after I got my new job, Cheryl got a nosebleed. I had to take her to the hospital. I got a bill for fifteen hundred dollars! I couldn't pay it. I had to quit my job so I could get my green card back.

"You know," I said, continuing my conversation with the Minnesota elder, "I bet if someone accused a farmer in your church of being lazy, as a reason for loosing his farm, he'd probably run him over with a tractor, right?"

He laughed. I laughed too, then I added, "My people get pretty upset when people who don't know them think they understand their problems, and worse yet, the solutions to them."

His eyes warmed. "You know," he said, "we may be a lot more alike than we are different."

Increasingly, farmers are finding it impossible to maintain dignity and livelihood through a hard day's work on a small piece of land. Mechanical, biological, and chemical revolutions in agriculture over the last fifty years have brought about a dramatic decline in the number of farm laborers. Economist and social critic Jeremy Rifkin argues that technological advancements in farming, further advanced by an economic system designed to reward only that which is large and highly profitable, has deprived millions of farmers from earning a livable wage.

Currently, more than nine million people living below the poverty line are living in rural America. Small farms are diminishing as our society has abandoned interest in the survival of anything small.

Chicago, 1997

While engaged in our spring ritual of pulling the weeds that climb our common fence, my neighbor responded to my inquiry about his new job, "Well, I fight traffic for three hours a day. The pay is lousy. I can do the job with my eyes closed. But it's a job and I'm lucky to have one."

John prides himself on being a hard worker. For fifteen years he worked at a neighborhood factory. With little notice the company moved south.

Struggling for a time on unemployment, John felt blessed when he found work at another neighborhood factory. A few years later he was "pink-slipped," as this company too migrated South, leaving him once again standing in an unemployment line. Two difficult years passed until he found a position as a security guard at a warehouse in a northern Chicago suburb.

"Where's the loyalty?" John asked. "You give a company your sweat for fifteen years, and you're treated like a piece of meat."

According to data from a 1993 Census Bureau report on poverty in America, the United States lost 1.6 million manufacturing jobs between 1989 to 1992, and the number of people living in poverty increased from thirty-one million to thirty-six million. In 1992, the top 0.5 percent of families owned 30.3 percent of household net worth, and the number of millionaires jumped to a record high, as did the number of billionaires.

Ironically, while millions live in poverty and are unemployed or underemployed, the amount of time working Americans spend on the job has risen steadily. In *The Overworked American*, Harvard economist Juliet Schor dismantles the popular myth that technology provides a higher quality of life and increased leisure time. In fact, working Americans have never worked harder or longer.

Citing research from sociologist Arlie Hochschild and economist Syliva Hewlet, Schor argues that the prosperity provided by our economic system is illusory. For example, half of U.S. marriages end in divorce. Many of those that have survived are close to the breaking point. While giving more time to their jobs, Americans are neglecting their marriages.

Perhaps more alarming is the effect that work obsession is having on our children. Studies show that child neglect has become endemic. Up to seven million children live in situations of "self care," or more accurately, no care. At least 500,000 preschoolers are left at home part of each day. According to a recent study, 911 operators are identifying an increasing number of frightened callers under the age of seven who have been left in charge of even younger siblings.

Indeed, our prosperity is illusory. Our economy has delivered a dramatically increased standard of living, but at a great cost. We have technological toys, but we depend on them to unwind after a stressful day at the office. We take vacations, but we work so hard through the year that they become indispensable to our sanity. We are literally working ourselves to death, as jobs contribute to heart disease, depression, hypertension, exhaustion, and a variety of other ailments.

Many of my students come to Chicago in the midst of studying to achieve this kind of "prosperity." I see their anxiety over what awaits them upon graduation, as they realize they will have to work extremely hard to find and maintain a lucrative career. During their Chicago semester they come to realize that a two-income family may be the only way to maintain the standard of living their parents provided them.

Added to this burden is the pressure to be successful and to make good on their parents' college investment. As they work at internships in their career fields, they see that they are likely to find themselves in a job that may hold little meaning, will demand sixty to seventy hours each week, and will require them to place their Christian principles on hold if they expect to move up the company ladder—a shaky ladder at best.

A student interning at a large Chicago corporation came to see me one afternoon. Through her tears, she explained that when she arrived at work, the employees in her department were solemnly placing their personal belongings into boxes. Her supervisor took her aside and said, "I'm sorry, but this department is no longer in operation. You'll have to pack your things and be out of the office by ten o'clock."

Farmers, factory workers, and now professionals are learning what the poor have known for some time—being unemployed has little to do with one's work ethic and much to do with an economic system that has abandoned an interest in anything small and whole. Christians are familiar with the Bible's warnings about money, but less familiar with the warnings about systems and the evil therein.

Recently I invited a Christian businesswoman to speak to my students. She genuinely wants to improve her employees' working conditions but faces an array of barriers. For example, if she deviates too much from the general norm for wages and benefits, competitors will simply price her out of business. Addressing a similar situation in his book *Engaging the Powers,* Walter Wink suggests that business persons need not be greedy—the system is greedy on their behalf. As he points out, most managers of Fortune 500 companies have had sensitivity training. The question is, Has the world noticed a difference?

While our economic system may be superior to others, it would be idolatrous for Christians to consider any system above the need for reform. Unfortunately, the principalities and powers wreak havoc not only on social systems, but also on belief systems.

In other words, the evil lies not only in the way we *do* economics but in the way we *view* economics. Our culture's belief system, or worldview, leads Christians to view economics as a game. If it is viewed in this way, notions like "winners and losers" and "killing the competition" make logical sense. Directed by rules supplied by the laws of economics, Christians and non-Christians play the same game, in the same way, without much distinction. Why? Because matters of faith and conscience are irrelevant to the game.

However, if we believe that what pretends to be a game is instead a holy activity, then we are positioned not only to acknowledge the ill effects our economic system has on the lives of both rich and poor, but also to reform the rules according to God's purposes. For the Christian, God's laws must always have primacy over economic laws.

The Bible tells us that God created the world, established and sustains the world, and calls humankind to govern the world through the creation of just systems. God's ways are loving ways. All arenas of life, including economics, are holy arenas.

Unfortunately, Christians have been duped into viewing our economic life as a practical science rather than a godly vocation. A student said it well: "We are taught to be good Christians when it comes to things like sex, but when it comes to work and money, we are taught to function as atheists."

If we continue in this vein, we may destroy the competition, but we will also destroy ourselves.

Chicago, 1990

During our congregation's prayer time, I asked the people to pray for me as I was beginning "D.Min." (Doctor of Ministry) studies. Eileen, a member of the church and a Lathrop resident, came over to me after the service. She took my hand and said in all earnestness, "I think it's wonderful that you are doing this demon program. I want you to know that I'll be praying for you because when you study demons, it's bound to really stir them up." When I tried to explain to Eileen what D.Min. stands for, she would hear nothing of my explanation. She remained convinced that my contribution, if it was to be significant, must involve the study of demons.

In fact, she was right. If we intend to do ministry in the twenty-first century, we had better study demons.

CHAPTER 8

Salvation

*If you remove the yoke from among you,
the pointing of thefinger, the speaking of evil, if
you offer your food to the hungry and satisfy the
needs of the afflicted, then your light shall rise in
the darkness and your gloom be like the noonday.
The Lord will guide you continually, and satisfy
your needs in parched places, and make your
bones strong; and you shall be like a watered
garden, like a spring of water, whose
waters never fail.*
—Isaiah 58:9b-11

Chicago, 1989

The workcamp group gathered on the floor of the converted tavern that at the time housed the ministry of the Church of the Good News. The campers were from one of the largest, most prestigious congregations in our denomination. The youth leaders had been given a night off, "on the town," so it was just twenty-five freshly showered, well-groomed, beautifully clad teenagers and me.

I asked them how things were going. They had been working hard refurbishing a few public housing apartments in ninety-degree weather, but it was their frame of mind that interested me. They gave me the usual "Oh, great!" and "Terrific!" and someone said, "You know, your idea about how to deal with the cockroaches really helped. Once we gave them names, it wasn't so bad!" (I had explained that naming the demons is always the first step in gaining power over them. It's what educators call "a teachable moment.")

But then something most interesting occurred. Rather than talking about the horrid conditions of the public housing development, the financial struggles and the physical and emotional abuse endured by the people with whom they were working, they began talking about their lives: their homes, their church, their pain. They described their church as, in their words, "an elitist social club."

"It's all about what you wear and what pew you sit in, if you ask me," one of the girls said.

The young people despaired about the absence of their parents from their lives, due to careers, and the lack of encouragement and support from them. Group members shared how their friends were turning to drugs and cults because there was little else that offered them much in terms of community.

Then one of the youths dared to say something that was very close to home for all of them. She said, "You know, Jimmy should be here with us."

The room turned quiet, and I noticed tears on the faces of these beautiful young people. Jimmy, I discovered, was a boy from their church who had committed suicide earlier that summer.

Eventually one of the youths broke the silence. "I don't think we're all that different from the kids in this neighborhood. Last night you said that they join gangs because they need a place to belong—that their families are pretty messed-up. You said that the kids who join gangs are really good kids, but have just given up on life. Jimmy gave up on life. He was hurting and none of us knew how badly."

Chicago, 1999
Kathy

Kathy works as an investment specialist for a Chicago firm. She is friendly and outgoing, assertive, but not too pushy. Actually, that may not be true. Sometimes I imagine she's quite pushy. The corporate world is not an easy world for a woman, but if someone will break the glass ceiling of corporate America, it's likely to be Kathy.

Kathy works hard for what she has, and she has a lot: a BMW, membership in an exclusive ski club and a local fitness center, and the latest electronic gadgets, including a cellular phone so small it can get lost in a shirt pocket. Her Lake Shore apartment is the envy of many.

"It's a beautiful place to live," she said to my students, "and there's good security too. Can't be too careful these days."

She's right about that. Many in our cities are in desperate situations.

Every morning at five o'clock Kathy jogs the lakefront path.

"Must keep fit," she said. "That gets me ready for the office."

After the jog, she cools down with the *Wall Street Journal* and a glass of juice before taking a shower and commuting to her downtown office. She used to drive her "Beemer" to work, but she's learned to settle for public transportation.

"Too easy to get dents with all the crazies out there. And the parking attendants are the worst!" she said.

Once in her office, it's all business. But she loves her work. Making money for people is a thrill for Kathy. Her job is to take other people's money and invest it in stocks and bonds. The interesting thing is, she can't lose.

"Whether there's a market gain or loss, a buy or sell, I make a commission," Kathy explained to my students. "Of course, if you want long-term clients, you would do well to know what you're doing."

In today's business world, however, few jobs or professional relationships last for long. "Here today and gone tomorrow. That's the reality out there."

She's right. It used to be that an employee might stay with one company for most of a career. On average, today's workers will be employed by seven different companies in the course of a lifetime. There used to be something called company loyalty—employers loyal to employees and vice versa. It's not so anymore, Kathy makes clear.

So she tries not to worry about long-term realities. She knows she'll soon be moving on to something else.

While Kathy understands that saving is a good idea, it's one that seems to fall by the wayside. Even though she makes good money, her bills rise like magic to the level of her income.

"Gotta cut up those credit cards," she said after a ski trip with a group of young professionals.

Kathy hasn't much by way of family. Her parents divorced when she was ten. She loves them but can't seem to handle being with them much. When they split up, she said, something broke inside her. When a student asked about her social life, she laughed.

"I haven't much time for that," she said.

"Not much sense of community around here," she continued, describing her Lake Shore neighborhood. "A lot of people are coming and going. They just don't stay very long."

She explained that companies transfer employees like any other commodity.

Kathy's best memory of apartment life is from a stormy Chicago night. People ran through the hallways, asking each other if they too had lost power. A pre-melt-down ice-cream social erupted in the hallway.

"It was great! Here we are, strangers eating each other's ice cream and sharing toppings. It was very cool," she said, as the memory brought a gleam to her eyes.

Linda

The interior of Linda's suburban home will take your breath away: colorful carpets, wall hangings hand quilted by Linda. And the paintings—both hers and her children's. Even the messiest, most childish compositions are displayed in such an attractive way that they look intentional, if not professional.

Linda left her profession years ago. It was a difficult decision. She was good at her work and could have been quite successful. But she wanted to be with her children.

Don't tell her she doesn't work, because she's likely to strike you down. Three children, a husband rarely home, a house to keep, volunteer commitments to fulfill—all keep her busy from five in the morning until ten in the evening, often later.

"I consider myself fortunate," she said to my students. "I can afford to be a stay-at-home mom. My husband makes good money and would be the first to say that I earn his paycheck every bit as much as he does."

Linda admits that it's difficult to feel like you're of equal worth when most of your day involves conversing with children who are between the ages of three and ten.

"I've lost a bit of my vocabulary, I'm afraid," she confessed.

But her husband tries to be supportive. "He will tell you that the best day of his life was the day I quit my job," Linda said, ungrudgingly.

Two-career couples with children may drool at the thought of having a full-time spouse at home taking care of housekeeping, childcare, and everything else that so often falls between the cracks of the typical American family. As John Cowan, author of a book on spirituality and the workplace writes, "If you really want to be successful in business *and* have a marriage and family, then you better get a 'wife.'" He places the word "wife" in quotation marks because whether you're a professional man or woman, you'll need a wife if you expect to be successful in today's workplace.

Linda is that wife. And a good one she is: loving, gentle, disciplined with her children, and patient with her husband. But she worries, mostly about her daughters.

"I want them to see me as more than a wife," she said. "I want them to know the parts of me that have died— the parts of me that I once knew so well—the parts that used to flourish 'out there.' "

Our darkness longs for noonday; our parched places for satisfaction.

Chicago, 1997

The call came from out of the blue. My memories of Brian had faded in the seven years since his semester in Chicago. But as we talked, I recalled his first classroom comment: "My goal is that by age thirty I will have earned my first million dollars."

His vehicle would be investment banking, and he expected his internship at the Chicago Board of Trade to provide his start. It did. He got close to the million-dollar mark in 1996. The reason for his call was to invite me to lunch as a way of thanking me for my role in his Chicago semester.

After the lunch table was cleared, he took out his semester journal, placed it on the table, and said, "Do you have any idea how angry your comments made me?"

I said, "I remember the week you wouldn't speak to me."

We laughed. He explained how difficult it was for him to attend the neighborhood visits where he was "forced" to talk with homeless people, public housing residents, and ex-convicts.

"Those events made me so mad. Everything I believed about the poor was challenged. Everything I had been taught to believe was under attack."

Brian said it took him a few years to sort through his Chicago experience, and that only a few months before our lunch did everything fall into place.

"My life was going according to my plan. I had the condo, the Lexus, and was close to my first million. But I was miserable."

Then Brian told me he had quit his job and enrolled in a master's degree program sociology at Western Michigan University. He said he is now looking to use his skills in a way that will make a difference.

"What I really want to do is teach. My mother's a teacher. Actually, I'm a lot like my mother."

Chicago, 1998

These comments are excerpted from a student paper:

This semester I learned a great deal about the city and myself. First of all, when looking at the homeless population, I never would have thought that so many of them had once held good jobs. Several of the people we talked with were intelligent and well educated. Before Chicago, I hadn't thought much about where these people come from. I just assumed they were lazy alcoholics and drug addicts.

I also changed my thinking toward the people who live in public housing. Clearly, most of the residents are not abusing welfare. Story after story told how the residents are trying to break free from public aid, but are stuck in a system that encourages them to stay dependent and poor.

I have volunteered in the past and want to volunteer in the future, but even this leaves me uncomfortable—it's like putting a Band-Aid on something that calls for surgery. The closing words of the woman on the public housing panel still ring in my ears: "Don't worry about us. We've got it goin' on over here. The best thing you can do for us is get your own house in order."

At first her words made me angry. Who is she to tell me I have problems, or that her problems have anything to do me? But I couldn't get her words out of my mind. And I know why. It's because I know she's right. I have to get my own life in order. I have to rethink why I want to give so much of my future time and energy to the world of advertising.

Why am I going to spend my life trying to convince people to buy things they don't need? Why am I going to convince people they need more and more things while so many people are struggling so hard to simply live?

Life would have been so much easier if I would have just stayed in Iowa this semester! Now I have to figure out what I'm going to do with my life. I'm glad I have another semester of school. I need time to think. I need time to pray.

Conclusion

I conclude with a story written by my wife, Reverend Liala Ritsema Beukema.

> She sits in the back of the church in the chair nearest the door. Even though she arrives before most people, one hardly notices her presence. If she is noticed, she is barely acknowledged in the hustle and bustle of the morning's activities. Clutched tightly to her chest is her tattered shopping bag—a precious satchel of her most valued possessions. Her dark hair, streaked with gray, seldom washed or properly combed, is tucked haphazardly under her knit beret. Scars, scabs, and sores are positioned about her face, making looking at her a difficult and unenchanting task.
>
> As you watch from a distance you see her lips move, forming words that are heard only by the angels that most certainly surround her imagination, for the space around her is visibly empty. If by chance you care to listen, or are compelled to listen for some practical purpose, you must bend close to her face—a motion you don't relish, for her appearance is quite disturbing and the smell from her body is definitely uninviting. Her voice is low and whispery, and her messages coded and incoherent, of little apparent relevance to the issues of the day.
>
> In those brief moments when you give her your attention, you wonder from where she has come. Your worst fears are imagined—she is ill, she is un-

speakable; she will touch you or your loved ones, or
worse yet, cause a disturbance to our morning's
worship. Yet the mystery of her coming or going
does not spur you or others toward discovery.
Instead we permit her quiet entrances and exits, un-
interrupted and unconnected. We dare not ask or
wonder who she is, why she is here, or what gift she
receives, for that requires interaction, or perhaps a
relationship.

She is the nameless woman. Homeless. Helpless.
Needy. We place ourselves above her. Measuring out
our pity for her condition, we distance ourselves
from her, for fear she will require more energy than
we are able or willing to give.

In our mind's eye, we have already categorized
her, analyzed her, and diagnosed her, without even
the slightest moment of care or conversation. Of
course we know her. We have seen hundreds like
her—on the street, in the subway, in doorways of
abandoned buildings, and we breathe a heavy sigh
at the thought of having to deal with what will most
certainly be a mountain of problems—the baggage
she has brought to us.

Gathering up your courage, you approach her,
although you are not yet committed. She reaches
out and touches your arm. For a second you look,
not into her eyes, but at the gnarled and crippled
hand that brushes your sleeve. *Look up,* you think
to yourself. *Look at her.* Her mouth begins its motion. *Closer. Get closer. Try and listen to what she is
saying.* "How's your father?" she whispers.

Your father? His heart attack was weeks ago.
Had she remembered? How had she heard? "I pray
for him everyday," she continues. A tear begins to

form in the corner of her eye. "My mother had the same thing. I'm praying for you."

In a second, you are saved. The barriers that separate you from her are down. That unfathomable chasm that existed has been bridged. Not that you yourself crossed it. Not that those of us with all our righteousness, opportunity, and power crossed the distance. No, we did nothing for our salvation. It was a gift—her gift to us. While we were about the business of exclusion, while we were conjuring up excuses and reasons to ignore her, keeping her nameless, she was praying for us. She knew our pain. She knew our vulnerability. She knew our name.

Isaiah claims that our thirst will be quenched if we do away with the yoke of oppression, the pointing of the finger, and the speaking of evil, and if we offer our food to the hungry and satisfy the needs of the afflicted. The connection the prophet makes between the poor and the affluent cannot be missed; both long for renewal that can only come through a relationship with each other and with God.

For the church to bring the gospel to our increasingly urban world, we need the eyes to see, the ears to hear, and the courage to cross our Jordon. Our salvation lies on the other side.

The Author

George D. Beukema was born in Roseland, a south-side Chicago neighborhood, but soon moved to Holland, Michigan, where his father attended college and seminary. Seven years later he moved to Cleveland, where his father accepted the call to serve a struggling inner city congregation. Richly blessed and challenged by this Cleveland experience as well as inspired by fond boyhood memories of Holland, Beukema eventually returned to this Michigan "tulip town." There he, like his father, attended Hope College and Western Theological Seminary and reflected on the meaning of his Cleveland experience and its significance for his vocation.

At Western Seminary, Beukema met Liala Ritsema, a student who shared his commitment to and passion for urban ministry. They married and soon after accepted a call to co-pastor an urban, multicultural congregation on Chicago's north side. They have two children, a daughter, Tessa, and a son, Jesse, who are a living testimony to the benefits of raising children in such an environment.

While serving the Chicago congregation, Beukema developed a program for providing urban service experiences to youth, college, and seminary groups, which he later organized as the Kingdom Bridge. Drawn to building bridges between urban and non-urban Christians, Beukema took a faculty position at the Chicago Metropolitan Center, a Christian college semester work-study program. There for ten years he developed and implemented a model for crosscultural urban education—a program enhanced through his D.Min. studies at Western Theological Seminary, where he intermittently taught a course on urban ministry.

Currently, Beukema is Director of Kingdom Bridge in Chicago and serves as a consultant to congregations in neighborhoods going through cultural and economic transition.